Never Give Up, Never Give In

Never Give Up, Never Give In

*How To Achieve
Your Goals Through
The Power Of
Perseverance*

by Bryan Drysdale and Julie Blau

SMD Publishing
Santa Cruz, CA

Cover design by Leslie Murray and DagWeiser
Book design by Leslie Murray
Edited by Erin Crook

Published by:
SMD Publishing
Santa Cruz, CA

Printed in the United States of America

Publisher's Cataloging in Publication Data
Drysdale, Bryan R. and Blau, Julie E.
Never Give Up, Never Give In: How to Achieve Your Goals
Through the Power of Perseverance
1. Self-Help - Goal Attainment, Perseverance 2. Psychology -
Personal Growth I. Title
93-086783
ISBN 0-9639506-7-3: $14.95 Softcover

Acknowledgments

Our gratitude to everyone who helped make this book possible, especially Erin Crook, Leslie Murray, Dag Weiser, Eleanor Drysdale, and Fran Soule.

Contents

Chapter 5: Developing Your Personal Power   107

Chapter 6: Operating In A *Tastes Good* Environment   135

for
Stephanie

*If one advances confidently in the
direction of his dreams, and endeavors
to live the life which he has imagined,
he will meet with a success unexpected
in common hours...*

—HENRY DAVID THOREAU

CHAPTER 1

The Power Of Perseverance

Two A.M. The pain startled him awake. Sharp pains were digging at his chest and shooting down his left arm. He knew what was happening but couldn't believe it. Heart attack. But he was only 36 years old—how could this be possible? He had been working hard, maybe too hard, but there had been no warning. His whole left side was becoming numb with pain.

There was no phone in his tiny room. The pain was getting worse. He was in the middle of a jungle and sure he was going to die. He left the room and crawled down to the local highway. By daybreak he was discovered by a passing public bus, and rushed to the hospital. Nearly unconscious with pain, he fell into full cardiac arrest and received last rites.

Five weeks later, actor Martin Sheen, fully recovered, returned to the set of Apocalypse Now *to resume his role as Captain Willard, the film's protagonist.*

Martin Sheen's heart attack in the Philippine Islands in March of 1977 was just one more misfortune in a seemingly endless parade of disasters that plagued director Francis Ford Coppola during the filming of Apocalypse Now. *Coppola endured setbacks that would have left most of us reeling and ready to quit. In the two years of principal filming, Coppola had to address and resolve countless difficulties, including the following:*

Original star Harvey Keitel was fired after just one week of filming. He was replaced with Martin Sheen.

Back home, Coppola received little support from Hollywood and from the U.S. government. This was the first major film about the Vietnam War at a time when many Americans were confused about the country's role in that war.

Their helicopters were seized in the middle of filming by the military to help quell a communist insurgency by rebels fighting for control of the Southern Philippine Islands.

Horrendous budget overruns forced Coppola to hock his entire personal estate, including his 22 room Victorian mansion in Northern California.

A disastrous typhoon struck the Philippines, leveling the set and forcing production to shut down for two months.

A key sequence in the film was jeopardized when Marlon Brando initially held out after receiving a million dollar advance, then showed up on the set hopelessly overweight.

Coppola had no idea how to end the film. He repeatedly discarded the suggestions of the writers, and had to

*convince the cast and crew to keep working on a movie
with no final scene.*

As costs became unmanageable, and the scope of problems with
the film continued to swell, Coppola never lost sight of his vision. His confidence confounded everyone who was involved with
the project. He refused to believe that the problems couldn't be
overcome, that the obstacles couldn't be removed. Early on, he
said, "I am going to make the movie, and if everyone knows I am
going to make the movie, everything else will fall into place....It's
not in the cards that we're not going to finish the movie." At the
time of Coppola's comments he had no idea the extent of the adversity he would face. But his initial attitude never wavered. He
was going to finish the film.

In August of 1979, Apocalypse Now opened to critical acclaim.
It eventually grossed 150 million dollars. The film claimed three
Golden Globes and two Oscars. Few projects have encountered
such difficulties and met with such success.

What is it that sustains us?

What is it that allows individuals like Francis Ford Coppola
to overcome seemingly insurmountable obstacles? What is
it that sustains people in times of change, doubt, and disappointment? Why are some blessed with an unflappable
resilience in the face of fear, frustrations, and setbacks, while
the rest of us usually buckle under such pressures? What
secret is possessed by those who seem to thrive on adversity that would defeat most of us?

There is one trait that Coppola possessed that was more
important than any other: perseverance. His ability to
persevere through difficult passages did not guarantee his

success, but its absence would have surely led to failure. Eventually, every significant pursuit is tested by adversity; in order to overcome the obstacles you will face, you must resolve to never give up, no matter what befalls you. This is the key that will ultimately determine your success or failure. *If you cannot persevere through adversity in the pursuit of your goals, you will not succeed.*

Always bear in mind that your own resolution to succeed is more important than any one thing.
—ABRAHAM LINCOLN

Every so often, a few individuals step forward out of the crowd, having grown tired of their place, and reestablish their boundaries. They become those things the rest of us only dream about. If you were to examine their accomplishments, what you would find common to all of them, without exception, is the willingness and the ability to persevere.

How do we find the endurance to keep going long after others have given up? There is no better teacher than experience. The best way to learn how to overcome setbacks is through trial by fire. We learn to face our fears only by confronting them. You cannot become resistant to adversity without first experiencing it.

By drawing on our resolve to succeed, to face life's challenges and come out on top, we can reverse our negative attitudes and focus on the abundance of opportunities that surround us. It is in this arena that we will find the strength to continue, the courage to face our fears, and the endurance to stay with a goal until we obtain all we desire.

There is a wealth of information available about how to set

our goals. But rarely does anyone tell us how to get through the difficult times, how to find the strength of character to persevere. How do we continue, when we most want to quit? How do we find the courage to put ourselves on the line, time after time, when most people are drawing back?

Learning the fundamentals that perseverance requires will give you the strength and endurance to succeed through all trial and adversity. You will rely on these principles again and again, as you set forth in pursuit of your goals. With perseverance, whatever you can dream, you can have.

THRIVING THROUGH ADVERSITY

*History records few careers which were not marked
in their early stages by inordinate, almost
superhuman difficulties and trials, calling
for immeasurable courage and faith.*

—EDWARD ACHESON

It is principles only that endure

Perseverance is the mental resolve to never give up and never give in. Truly successful people manage to persevere despite setbacks, and work until they reach their goals. No matter how many challenges they face, they eventually prevail. These are people who have decided what it is they want and accept nothing less than the realization of their goal.

Self-improvement techniques come and go, but it is principles only that endure. Success in most ventures can be quantified and copied. What is missing is the ability for most of us to see our ventures to the end. We are always searching for a device that will give us instant success; what we are missing is the realization that with tenacity and endurance, *all* of our goals are attainable.

Taking action in the face of adversity is a trait of confident, results-oriented people who refuse to settle for anything less than the realization of their dreams. Some people will take longer than others to get there; certain goals require more time and effort than others. But ultimately, it is the individuals who engage themselves to the best of their abilities when faced with challenges who succeed.

Perseverance is developed over time

All highly successful people draw on their strength of perseverance often. No great feat or accomplishment has ever been completed without someone first pushing through times of doubt and fear and frustration. Those who do push through these barriers develop a resolution to succeed that is so strong that when difficulties present themselves, they proceed with a renewed sense of confidence and commitment that carries them through all future challenges.

Adversity has the effect of eliciting talents which in prosperous circumstances would have lain dormant.

—HORACE

This is not something unique that successful people are born with; perseverance is like a muscle that is strengthened over time, with repeated exercise and effort. Persevering through difficult times builds a strength and a tolerance that allows you to ultimately succeed.

You can practice perseverance by refusing to quit. By persisting in the face of adversity you will develop an inner resolve that you can call on again and again when faced with challenges. Staying with your goals and working through repeated setbacks will set you apart from the crowd. As you find your successes growing and your dreams drawing ever closer, the confidence that you cultivate enables you to pursue increasingly challenging goals.

Persisting in the face of adversity means hanging in there when you find yourself alone during times of frustration and despair, when all you have to keep yourself going is the vision of the goal that brought you there. You may become exhausted in your struggle, but never allow this to dampen your spirit. Let challenges and defeat lend you the inspiration and strength to continue.

Tolerance to adversity is simply a state of mind. We can, at any time, make the decision to pursue our goals and not to quit, no matter what. Armed with an unflagging desire to persevere in the face of all adversity, you will eventually reach your goal. If you believe you will not quit no matter what befalls you, no matter how difficult your circumstances become, you have all that you will need to successfully obtain your goal.

> *...the healthy person...has a lot of problems, many of which he has deliberately chosen with the sure knowledge that in working toward their solution, he will become more the person he would like to be.*
> —NICHOLAS HOBBS

Adversity is a sign of effort

If you are not experiencing any degree of adversity then you are probably operating well beneath your potential. It could be that you are playing it too safe, setting goals that fail to challenge you. Goals that require little effort on your part are realized less often than substantial, more desired goals, because the lack of commitment and desire can easily thwart your efforts.

The absence of adversity also suggests a minimum of effort; little can be accomplished when your effort is low. By engaging in activities that create obstacles—obstacles that originate because of the magnitude or complexity of your goals, rather than from sloppiness—you can make dramatic leaps in your progress. The presence of adversity suggests that you are putting forth the necessary effort to reach your goals.

THE FUNDAMENTALS OF PERSEVERANCE

*The most important thing in life is to have great
aim and to possess the aptitude and the
perseverance to attain your objective.*

—GOETHE

Perseverance is coping with your problems

Perseverance is an inner strength, a strength of character, courage, and resolve. We will achieve our goals through a focused, continuous application of effort and a willingness to endure setbacks along the way. Perseverance is evidence of our commitment to our goals. It involves a particular state of mind, as well as competence in the use of specific tools or devices. Every skill or attribute required to achieve your goals can be learned, developed, or improved.

Your actions and behaviors determine what and who you are. You are not separate from your actions. If you want to define yourself in a particular way, you need to behave in a manner consistent with that model.

Constant application and repeated efforts is what produces results, and, ultimately, success. Our inability to accept this often causes us to give up too soon. Through careful planning and a ruthless attitude toward action you can fulfill the desires in your life. As you progress toward your goals, your capacity to sustain longer and more intense periods of work increases, and this in turn produces greater results.

Almost without exception, if we fail to attend to our problems when they present themselves, they do not go away.

Instead, they multiply, both in number and in difficulty. We are then faced with an increased number of more severe problems. By learning to cope with problems as we encounter them, we can achieve our greatest goals. Dr. George Sheehan, in his book Personal Best, says it this way: "Coping means to take the initiative, to strike back, to take charge, to dominate. When we cope, we are in control—we are masters of the situation." Coping with our problems, then, requires more than just acknowledging and accepting them. If we want to succeed, we must overcome our problems as they present themselves, through strength of purpose and perseverance.

Let him be not too eager to grasp some badge or reward and omit the work to be done. True success is in the doing.

— EMERSON

It's quite normal to be afraid of adversity. We tend to commit tremendous amounts of time and energy complaining about, trying to avoid, or making excuses for the problems and obstacles we face. These actions are unproductive for two reasons: first, complaining, avoiding, or making excuses for our problems never solves them. We are much better served by directing our efforts toward the solution or conquest of the obstacles we face. Second, adversity is inevitable—if our goals are substantial, and if we are working toward them, we will surely encounter difficulties.

Learn the fundamentals of perseverance

Perseverance is a state of mind. As such, it can be developed and improved. Perseverance is based on four fundamentals. As fundamentals, the absence of even one can prevent you from ever achieving the goals you want in your life. High achievers develop perseverance by:

- *Selecting significant goals* whose accomplishment rests at the edge of their abilities. They set well defined, worthwhile goals, and the pursuit of those goals is a celebration of their success.

- *Making a strong commitment* to those goals. Commitment to worthy goals provides the ambition to take action. An unwavering commitment will fuel your energy and keep you from quitting.

- *Developing the personal power* needed to obtain their goals. They focus exclusively on the tasks that lead to those goals. We must look to our personal power to help us determine the actions that will lead to our goal, and then empower us to stick with those tasks until we succeed.

- *Creating an environment* that facilitates the goal achievement process. To obtain success, we must always be creating the conditions and circumstances that will maximize our efforts and endurance. Your environment should nurture, empower, and inspire you.

THE POWER TO ACHIEVE

Desire is the starting point of all achievement...not a hope, not a wish, but a keen pulsating desire which transcends everything....Dreams are not born of indifference, laziness, or a lack of ambition.

—NAPOLEON HILL

Take control of your life

The power to take and maintain control over our lives resides in all of us. Whenever we exert this control over ourselves, we can rise to the challenges that face us and build the confidence we need to secure our success. The greater the effort you exert, the larger the goal you can accomplish. Begin simply with the desire to be successful, then define your desire. Your resolve to succeed will drive your efforts.

Success is assured the moment you fully understand that you are in control of your life, of the goals you attain, and of the failure you experience. It is possible for you to have the life you imagine, once you learn to concentrate your efforts and abilities in the direction of your choice.

What is it you want to do with your life? What is preventing you from doing what it is you want to be doing? The answer to these questions will tell you why you are not achieving these things. The questions are easy, but the answers are difficult. Finding the correct answers requires looking deep into your motives. If you possess the courage to seek the truth, nothing is beyond your reach.

When you start waking up in the morning with the belief

that your success is self-determined, that your future rests upon the actions you take, you have acquired all the power you need to get you where you want to go. Be sure you have chosen your destination with care; nothing is less productive and less satisfying than pursing goals that are not important to you. In order to pursue our greatest dream, we must take responsibility for our success.

While the future is the source of possibilities, it is in the behaviors of the present that a dream will or will not be made a reality.

—LESLIE CAMERON-BANDLER

Find your successful side

Begin with what you are trying to accomplish. Most of us want to find our successful side, the part of us that works hard, that works smart, that always seems to know what to do next—*and then does it.* Look past your fears; it is there that you will find the strength, power, and character to succeed.

If you wish to promote constructive changes in your life, you must consider the following points:

- *It will take time.* Be patient; your dreams cannot be rushed.

- *It will take determination.* Be resolute; your tenacity will be tested again and again.

- *You must make choices.* Be decisive; you can control your fate by the choices you make.

- *You must take risks.* Be bold; you must be willing to test your potential.

If you want something, you must be willing to take a risk.

If you *really* want something, you must to be willing to risk everything. Don't ever believe that the goals you desire are beyond your reach. They may be difficult to achieve and require years of work and sacrifices greater than you can now imagine, but if you can vividly envision their attainment, you can have them.

Your life will finally change for the better when you become more afraid of being nothing than of failing. Don't end up being more sorry for what you didn't do than for what you did do.

Either suffer the pain of discipline or the pain of regret.

—JIM ROHN

Today's challenge rests with doing the best you can, not sometimes, but every day. The challenge increases as your abilities improve, drawing out your best efforts. Half the work is finding your limits, and the other half is raising above those limits. We risk failure when we seek to surpass our limits, but failure at a specific task does not have to lead to failure in life. We fail in life only when we don't try. Prepare today for tomorrow's challenges, and always aim as high as your dreams suggest.

Meet adversity with perseverance

Each new level of accomplishment you reach will contain new problems, obstacles, and potential for setbacks that will invoke higher degrees of fear and uncertainty than anything you have previously experienced. When adversity arises:

• Acknowledge the obstacle that is before you. Do not ignore or try to go around it. The sooner you recognize the problem, the sooner you can fix it.

- Determine exactly what the problem is, and immediately make efforts to fix it; don't waste any time bemoaning your misfortune.

- Don't be afraid to make changes, even big changes, to your plan of action. Be sure any changes you make come from a clear evaluation of your progress, not from an emotional reaction to having hit a barrier.

Some men give up their designs when they have almost reached the goal, while others, on the contrary, obtain a victory by exerting at the last moment, more vigorous efforts than ever before.

—HERODOTUS

- Realize that some problems just can't be solved. But also understand that all problems can be *re*solved. Learn to tell the difference.

- Immediately move on, once the problem has been resolved. Make no excuses. Concentrate only on the next step that needs to be taken. Do not let unexpected problems dissolve your momentum.

Our goals can take years to reach, and they will require patience, commitment, and perseverance. There are no magical secrets or short-cuts. Our goals are pursued and obtained through hard work and consistent application. While everyone encounters obstacles, successful people have learned that the ability to persevere through adversity is the most important tool they possess. As long as you have the will to continue, you keep your goals within reach.

Developing perseverance is a lifetime task that requires

commitment to a goal, desire, patience, and a never-ending belief in yourself and your abilities. It will always be worth the effort.

CHAPTER 2

Defining Success

WHAT DOES SUCCESS MEAN TO YOU?

I must decide what I am going to do and what I am going to be. To do that, I must come to terms with myself and define what I believe, what I esteem, and what I truly and rightly detest.

—GEORGE SHEEHAN

Success is a state of mind

The idea of success confounds most of us. We want many things, but have a hard time identifying exactly what they are. Some define success as the accumulation of material goods. Some see it as the acquisition of power. Many think success is a distinction that will be bestowed on them when they reach some future milestone. But true success is none of these things.

Success is an abstract idea with numerous definitions. Success is first a state of mind. If you believe that you are successful, then you are. Success does not require power, position, or material possessions. The accrual of these things does not make you successful any more than their absence makes you a failure.

If you feel successful, you will act successful, and the natural result of this is the attainment of all you desire, both tangible and intangible. Your success and happiness should not depend on *any* particular outcome. In *Awaken The Giant Within*, Anthony Robbins states that "...the truth is that nothing has to happen in order for you to feel good...as long as we structure our lives in a way where our happiness is dependent upon something we cannot control, then we will experience pain." The key to developing a state of mind that facilitates goal achievement is to focus on those things that we can control, and eschew the rest.

Successful people know that they must possess peace of mind *before* they begin to pursue any particular goal; we must never believe that any one goal will bring us happiness. While dissatisfaction with our current situation can motivate us toward our goals, dissatisfaction with ourselves signals a problem that will not be remedied with the attainment of a single goal. First, find contentment with yourself; then, strive for greatness.

Do what you love, and success will follow

Success is a process—a process of ongoing improvement and fulfillment. The surest measure of success rests with your ability to work on tasks of your choosing. If you are doing the things you want to be doing, and enjoying them, then you are successful. Success begins with a goal and ends with a goal *pursued*. Success is the quest for achievement, not the achievement itself.

Peak performers say success is the capacity to feel good, to embrace happiness on a regular basis. What is it that will bring you happiness? What is it—exactly—that you want to be doing? Determine this, and you will have defined your success.

Develop goals that inspire you. Make them personal. Do not choose a goal that you think will please someone else—you will not succeed. You are the only one who can decide what will bring you the most fulfillment. By recognizing that everyone's personal definition of success is different, we are free from having to compare ourselves to the achievements of others, and to the expectations that others have for us.

You must first be who you really are, then do what you need to do, in order to have what you want.
—MARGARET YOUNG

The daily pursuit of inspiring, personal goals is the ultimate expression of success. By pursuing a goal with passion and determination, the outcome becomes secondary, and the pursuit is everything. Success comes when you are transforming good ideas into action, turning intangible dreams into tangible results.

Look at the people around you, and identify the ones who you consider to be successful. What are they doing with their lives? How do they spend their time? Are they actively pursuing or engaging in something they enjoy?

What traits seem to be common to all of these people? Set

your own goals, but do not hesitate to emulate the habits and actions of other people who are succeeding.

What others have said...

There are many ways to define success. The common denominator is the personal aspect. An ideal method for developing a better understanding of success is to examine the definitions provided by successful people in the fields of writing, sports, motivation, and politics.

Earl Nightingale, motivational speaker:

"Success is the progressive realization of a worthy ideal or goal."

Denis Waitley, writer:

"...attitude is the criterion for success. Your attitude toward your potential is either the key to or the lock on the door of personal fulfillment."

Henry David Thoreau, essayist:

"If the day and the night are such that you greet them with joy, and life emits a fragrance like flowers and sweet-scented herbs, is more elastic, more starry, more immortal—that is your success."

Mary Robinson, writer:

"Developing success means focusing less on loss and more on parlaying already existing success."

Tom Hopkins, sales trainer:

"Success isn't all of a sudden—success is every day."

Rita Davenport, writer:

"Successful people get into the habit of success. They learn how to have a success experience and then repeat the experience again and again and again."

Richard M. Nixon, former president:

"Success is not a harbor but a voyage with its own perils to the spirit. The game of life is to come up a winner, to be a success, or to achieve what we set out to do. Yet there is always the danger of failing as a human being. The lesson that most of us on this voyage never learn, but can never quite forget, is that to win is sometimes to lose."

Bob Dylan, songwriter:

"A man is a success if he gets up in the morning and gets to bed at night and in between does what he wants to do."

John Thompson, basketball coach, Georgetown University:

"To know yourself. That's the secret of success. To know what you want and have the confidence to define your world, your goals, and your achievements on your own terms."

Art Linkletter, television personality:

"Success is a journey, not a destiny. It should be enjoyed through the entire trip, not endured until the final reward."

Ralph Waldo Emerson, essayist:

"I look on that man as happy, who, when there is the question of success, looks into his work for a reply."

THE FUNDAMENTALS OF SUCCESS

The most valuable result of all education is to make you do the thing you have to do, when it ought to be done, whether you like it or not; it is the first lesson that ought to be learned; and however early a man's training begins, it is probably the last lesson that he learns thoroughly.

—THOMAS HUXLEY

You already know what success requires

No one can teach you how to be successful. Success is the natural result of adhering to certain principles or fundamentals, and is attained by choosing and moving forward toward your goals. It requires a dream, an obsession for the dream, and time spent in quiet contemplation developing a plan to obtain your dream. Success also requires hard work. It requires persisting when you are tired and persevering when you are tempted to quit. It also requires the serenity to enjoy and appreciate your goals when they finally becomes yours.

It doesn't matter how ambitious you are, which gimmick or get-rich-quick scheme you pursue. Without a basic understanding of success, an ability to assess your progress and to make adjustments as needed, and, most importantly, the endurance to persevere, you will likely end up no closer to your goals than you are today.

Success is achieved through the consistent application of numerous fundamentals whose benefits accumulate over time. When other people are enjoying benefits that you desire, you can be sure that it is possible for you to enjoy them, too. Those who have achieved the success you are chasing are simply making different decisions than you are. These decisions include where they direct their attention, where they focus their energy, and what actions they take on a daily basis to achieve their goals.

The habits of high achievers

Success is rarely dependent on the skills or talents with which you begin. It comes from practicing certain principles and maintaining a positive, goal-oriented attitude. If you want something deeply enough, you must commit yourself to its attainment, work hard at its achievement, remain positive, and never give up. Learn the traits that are common to all high achievers, and practice them in your life.

Successful people:

- *Are ambitious.* They possess extraordinary drive and determination. Their goals are lofty, and the desire to reach those goals is the catalyst for their efforts.

- *Are skillful problem-solvers.* They approach their problems in such a way that the solution benefits their goals, reduces the chances of the problem reoccurring, and prevents the solution from creating new problems. Peak performers also go to great lengths to be sure they're working on the right problem.

- *Do what is necessary.* They know that any significant accomplishment requires that you do what needs to be done, when it's time to do it. Successful people act on their intellect, not on their impulses.

- *Are influenced by the desire for pleasing results,* as opposed to the desire for pleasing methods. They are willing to make sacrifices to reach their goals. High achievers know that the price of success includes making difficult choices.

- *Stay focused.* They know that it's impossible to travel in two directions simultaneously. They understand that they are either moving forward toward success or backward toward failure. Successful people concentrate only on the work at hand.

- *Are industrious.* They have a bias for daily action and a compulsion toward closure. They try to accomplish something every day, and always finish what they start.

- *Are optimistic.* They believe they will achieve success. They favor one of the following outlooks in life: That good events will happen, or that bad events won't. They know that maintaining an optimistic outlook helps to overcome obstacles and makes total defeat an impossibility.

- *Are able to work in the midst of fear.* They know that where there is fear, there is also the power to face and overcome fear and do what's necessary. Successful people never allow their fears to become greater than their commitment to their goals.

- *Are patient.* Winners understand that success takes time. They know that seeking and expecting immediate results creates excessive anxiety and inhibits creative energy. They know that the search for immediate gratification is a killer of dreams.

- *Know that success breeds success*, just as failure breeds failure. When they make progress, they feel good about themselves; when they feel good about themselves, they make more progress. This creates a cycle of success.

- *Have high self-esteem.* The belief that they are worthy of their goal guides them through difficult passages, and gives them faith to continue.

- *See success as a process, motion, movement, or action—not a result, place, position, or thing.* Successful people know that it's the movement toward a meaningful and significant goal that creates success.

Decide to make positive changes

There are two things to aim at in life: first, to get what you want; and, after that, to enjoy it.
—LOGAN PEARSALL SMITH

You can take control of your life by sim-ply making the decision to do so. You are the only one who can change your atti-tude, your lifestyle, your goals. Many of us make the mistake of believing that if we could change our environment, or if we could only change the behavior of the people in our lives, we would be on our way to success and happiness. But without changing our own behaviors and attitudes, there will be no change at all.

There are many positive changes you can make today that will put you on the road toward achieving your goals. On any given day, you can choose to change something about the way you live. It can be as small an act as organizing your long-neglected desk, or something as significant as letting go of a self-destructive habit.

Make a resolution to yourself that you will keep moving forward toward your goal, that you will see your dream realized. Make a solemn promise to yourself that you will succeed. Any resolution or decision we make is worthless until we have formed the habit of making that promise, and keeping it. You must have a strong, overriding purpose that inspires you to keep the promises you make to yourself.

Developing successful habits requires diligent practice. Any resolution made today must be made tomorrow, the next day, and the day after that, until it becomes routine. Practice developing the traits that come easy to you, to build your confidence, competency, and endurance. Deliberate action must be taken to create good habits, or bad habits will develop instead. Negative habits form readily in the presence of a vacuum.

> *There is nothing training cannot do. Nothing is above its reach. It can turn bad morals to good; it can destroy bad principles and recreate good ones; it can lift men to angelship.*
>
> —MARK TWAIN

The desire for your goal must become so intense that you literally do not recognize or accept any result other than the realization of that goal. But never think that the desire for success alone will bring your goal to you. You must also be willing to work tirelessly toward the attainment of your goal, and make the sacrifices required of you.

Winners develop the habit of overcoming the obstacles they encounter en route to their goals. They know obstacles will appear, but rarely worry about them in advance, choosing instead to deal with problems as they occur. This doesn't mean that they ignore potentially damaging situations; rather, high achievers do what they can to influence those things over which they have control, and do not waste their energy trying to change what they cannot control.

Begin at once putting the fundamentals to work in your life by maintaining your focus on forward movement, positive results, desired outcomes, and favorable endings. Develop the traits of the highly successful, and your own success will follow.

THERE IS NO FAILURE SAVE QUITTING

Few things are impracticable in themselves. Most things fail not for want of means, but simply because of lack of application.

—DE LA ROCHEFOUCAULD

Failure is the inability to discipline yourself

Failure is often defined as the inability to achieve a goal. But who says when we have failed? We fail only when we give up in the pursuit of our goals, when we stop working toward our personal definition of success—or worse, if we never begin. Failure, then, is the inability to discipline yourself to do what must be done.

No matter how long it takes you to reach your goal, or how many setbacks you endure, as long as you are still working in some way toward the achievement of your goal, you have not failed. Failures are people who know what they want and how to get it, but do little or nothing to achieve it.

The problem rests not in our lack of understanding of what needs to happen, but rather in our unwillingness to do the work. It's always easier to sit there and not participate. Define your success and embrace a ruthless attitude toward self-disciplined behavior.

Once you understand how to achieve success, you no longer look for short cuts. Instead, you look for the best way to accomplish your task. Regardless of the prospect of initial setbacks, your resiliency develops into a strong resolve, capable of guiding you past any barriers you might encounter.

Most of us want success and the gifts it promises. But when

the critical time arrives—when we either take action or hesitate—the majority of us run for cover, leaving in our wake a host of excuses and rationalizations. Quitting robs us of the opportunity to see ourselves at our best, and we will never succeed if we can't develop the perseverance to see our ventures through to the end.

The average person finds it much easier to quit than to continue. We have learned that it's okay to give up on our goals if the pursuit becomes too difficult, or if we cannot succeed overnight. Why work sixty hours a week to build a business you believe in, when you might win the lottery tomorrow? Why spend years in school when you might become a rock star overnight? We're obsessed with quick riches and the pursuit of instant gratification. We live an environment that favors the pursuit of tension-relieving activities at the expense of worthy goals. Too often, when the road becomes difficult or uncomfortable, we simply quit.

Losers visualize the penalties of failure. Winners visualize the rewards of success.
—Dr. Rob Gilbert

Most people quit because they are unwilling or unable to persevere. At some point the will to obtain the goal ceases to be enough to sustain the necessary effort. Giving up is the path of least resistance. Quitting takes the pressure off and even provides a temporary sense of relief. But relief soon gives way to dissatisfaction and regret, as we find ourselves no closer to our goals.

Once you realize that you are in complete control of your success or failure, you will be less inclined to quit. The development of your personal power will help you overcome the obstacles you face. Continue to apply time and effort toward your important goals, no matter how long it takes or what difficulties you come up against.

Setbacks are temporary—failure is permanent

Encountering setbacks while pursuing your goals is natural and inevitable. No one can chart the perfect path to their goals. You will come across obstacles previously unforeseen. Often these obstacles will appear to be greater than your capacity to overcome them. This is where most of us despair, not understanding why things are going wrong. This is the critical point on your path. Instead of quitting, gather your resources and do the best you can, letting the outcome develop as it will. Take control of the things you can control, and keep moving forward.

There is a real difference between failing and being a failure. The loser isn't the one who comes in last—it's the one who never entered the race.

—HARRY CORDELLOS

Suffering a temporary setback or defeat while in pursuit of your goal is just another step in the learning process. Each step is important for developing the set of skills you will need. Each one must be taken before the next; trying to circumvent this process will only sabotage your efforts. Taking shortcuts because you are impatient or unwilling to do the necessary work will only lead to shallow achievements, and any gains you make will quickly be lost.

Temporary setbacks may imply defeat, but they don't have to equal failure. Understanding failure prevents you from ever committing the greatest act of failure there is—saying, "I've had enough and can't do this any longer." Unless you've given up, you have not failed. You can recover from any setback, save quitting.

A temporary setback can seem devastating. Being turned down by the bank for a loan that is essential to your business may appear to mark the end, but until you've decided that it's over, it's not. By taking the time to generate new ideas, you might be able to come up with a solution that will allow your business to remain afloat. There are always creative options open to those who search them out, such as borrowing money from private sources, bringing in investors, or negotiating with your creditors. Most people are so crushed by the first big defeat they suffer that they give up before exploring all of their options. As long as the desire to make a success of your business remains strong, you will find a way to keep the doors open.

Set in your mind that you will succeed, and do not allow yourself to accept failure as an outcome. Adversity is inevitable, losses will occur, but total failure only takes place if you allow it. You need only set your goals, go to work achieving them, and never accept any result other than the attainment of your goal. View temporary setbacks as simply that—temporary. To keep your dream alive, you must never give up, never stop your progress.

Failure is not an option

As long as we refuse to accept failure as an option, we can never lose. Only when we perceive ourselves as losers have we lost. You can lose at a game of tennis without being a failure as a tennis player. This may appear to be a subtle difference, but it's the crucial distinction between success and failure, between winning and losing.

There will be setbacks. Unforeseen problems of varying degrees will visit us. We will lose our best clients, blow the interview, injure ourselves. But by examining what we did wrong—as well as what we did right—we can learn from our experiences and carry this knowledge into future ventures.

Men don't fail; they give up trying.

—ELIHU ROOT

We will encounter many defeats before we attain our bigger goals, and we will continue to experience setbacks as long as we are active in the pursuit of achievement. Peak performers understand this and use this knowledge to their advantage by remaining firm in their resolve to never give up. They don't quit when confronted by initial setbacks, and this attitude distances them from everyone else. We must not quit before we discover what we are capable of achieving.

PERSEVERANCE—THE BEST DEFENSE AGAINST FAILURE

History has demonstrated that the most notable winners usually encountered heartbreaking obstacles before they triumphed. They won because they refused to become discouraged by their defeats.

—B.C. FORBES

Perseverance prevents failure

As long as you continue to persevere, you are preventing failure. Although you may meet with temporary setbacks, disappointments, and rejections, you must counter them with resolve and determination. Let adversity be a challenge to you; the more obstacles you overcome, the more satisfying your success will be.

Remember that you are the only one who can make the decision to quit or to continue, to keep moving forward or to give up as you may have done in the past. Only you can say when the battle is over, and only you can decide if you've lost. Taking total responsibility for your successes and failures provides you with the power and endurance that you need to reach your goals.

When times appear most difficult, bear in mind that you are much more resilient than you think. Most of us have overcome obstacles that, at the time we initially faced them, seemed insurmountable. Each time we push through a barrier and come out on the other side, we renew our confidence and strengthen our ability to face the next challenge.

Success is the ultimate manifestation of perseverance. Your

success is evidence of your ability to persevere, and possessing this trait is like always having the correct answer, regardless of the question. With this kind of confidence at your disposal, no goal is beyond your reach.

If you persevere through the difficult times, you will ultimately succeed. At any point, we can resolve to endure adversity and meet our challenges head-on, or we can quit. We can choose to be successful—or we can choose to fail. There is no greater success than success that has met with difficulty, and continued on.

CHAPTER 3

Setting Your Goals

GREAT PURSUITS BEGIN WITH GREAT DREAMS

*Success is the achievement of a goal, and without
goals there can be no successes...half of success
is simply noticing it.*

—GREGG LEVOY

Goals not set are seldom attained

Goal setting is predicated on the idea that you will achieve only those dreams that you attempt to achieve. Forget about luck, fate, or destiny. If you want something, you must take responsibility for getting it. If you *really* want something, then you are obligated to do whatever it takes—barring the unethical or illegal—to get it. Conceive your goals, then set about obtaining them. Goals not set are seldom attained.

All great pursuits begin with great dreams. We must not be afraid to pursue what our instincts tell us we can achieve. Opportunities are always present in one form or another; we do not have to look very far to find an undertaking that is worthy of our time and effort.

Most of us have great ideas, but little notion how to pursue them. Without a goal, there will be no direction to follow, no way to measure your progress. Although you may believe at a conscious level that you want to be successful, unless you first define what success means to you, the achievement of that success is impossible.

First say to yourself what you would be and then do what you have to do.

—EMERSON

Decide that you *should* live your dream, believe that you *can* have it, resolve that you *will* achieve it. Then begin. Where you begin is not important, what matters is that you start *now*.

Goals are the source of our inspiration

Anthony Robbins has written and lectured extensively about success and the value of goal setting. In *Awaken The Giant Within*, he discusses the importance of goals: "Setting goals is the first step in turning the invisible into the visible—the foundation for all success in life." It is here—creating the foundation—that we must begin, for without the strongest foundation, we will have nothing to fall back on when problems arise.

Engage in pursuits that are worthy of your efforts. Be sure your goals are worthwhile; they must provide you with the inspiration, strength, and stamina to overcome the adversity that will confront you on the road to your success. You cannot put forth the effort or create the motivation—day in and day out—with willpower alone. You need a goal that transcends your daily life and problems, a goal that inspires you to work toward it until it is realized.

Goals can provide structure in your life when times are tough. When faced with difficult situations, your goals can *ground* you and provide a stabilizing influence in your life. As your goals are the source of your inspiration, they must be deeply rooted in your greatest dreams. They must become an anchor to which you can attach your hopes.

Don't be afraid to take a big step if one is indicated. You can't cross a chasm in two small jumps.
—David Lloyd George

You will gain strength only from a goal so compelling that it inspires you to complete it. Be sure to choose goals that instill in you both inspiration and desire. You will need to draw from these sources often, especially when your resolve is challenged.

For some of us, the desire to achieve a set goal is the sole motivation. For others, it is the financial or social reward that success promises. Still others are fueled by a sense of challenge, by a desire to complete a difficult task. The source of your inspiration is unimportant, but your motivation must be unshakable, and you must be able to sustain it when you are beset by inevitable adversity.

Do not allow the potential loftiness of your goal to keep you in awe. Setting and pursuing challenging goals allows you to accomplish tasks that you once considered out of reach. The pursuit of important goals brings with it the ability to achieve them. Because it is challenging and important to you, your goal will elicit your best efforts. A sure indication that you are heading in the right direction is when you notice that tasks have become commonplace that once seemed difficult.

Identify the ideal action

The optimum result of goal setting is the creation and implementation of the ideal action. What constitutes an *ideal action*? Doing the right thing at the right time. While this concept is simple in theory, in practice it's never easy. It's simple because you know what is the right thing to do, and when is the right time to do it. This knowledge is instinctive. Many of us ignore our instincts, because often, doing the right thing at the right time is the hardest task that presents itself each day.

We must do difficult things if we are to succeed. By keeping in touch with our instincts and maintaining an awareness of the ideal action, we always know which is the correct path to take. Each time we act on a deliberate, conscious decision, we move closer to our goal.

Some of us have trouble identifying the ideal action, while others are unable to act on it. Modern-day philosopher Dr. George Sheehan feels that each and every one of us "...is capable of the ideal or moral action....Anyone so inclined can decide on ideal action." The task then is to discover what our version of the ideal action is, put aside all other irrelevant activities, and take the first step toward it.

The ideal action is what we are always searching for—either attempting to discover what it consists of, or, that ascertained, finding the motivation to carry it out. What other use of our time could be more important, more pressing, than the pursuit of actions that lead us to our dreams? This is where your goals become motivators—they bridge the gap between what you know you should do, and doing it.

Do what you love. Pursue what most interests you. Set goals that always culminate in the attainment of those things you want. Move from wishing to wanting to getting. Wishing is a vague daydream that rarely results in action. By intensifying your wishes into a desire to obtain what you covet, you set in motion the actions that will result in the realization of your greatest dreams.

A man should conceive of a legitimate purpose in his heart, and set out to accomplish it. He should make this purpose the centralizing point of his thoughts.

You already possess the intelligence and good conscience required to know right from wrong. You know at an instinctive level exactly what it is that you should be doing with your life. You also have the strength to act on the correct choice,

—JAMES ALLEN

whether or not you are aware of this. Each time you make the right choice, it will be easier to do so again at the next opportunity. In the same way, each time you make a decision that is detrimental to your best interests, you reinforce that behavior. Every time you make a decision to act in a manner appropriate to the type of person you want to become, you make it easier to behave in that manner in the future.

Most of who you are and what you do is a product of your experience. Despite this, you still operate from a free will;

the decisions you make with respect to the choices you face will always be yours. Daily you encounter opportunities to make decisions that will allow you to improve yourself and your environment, or cause you to regress. There are no neutral choices; we are either moving closer to or further from our goals.

Set goals that inspire you to achieve them

In the divine account books, only our actions are noted, not what we have read or what we have spoken.

—GANDHI

Often the problem lies not in our unwillingness to pursue our goals, but rather in the quality of our existing goals. We are always in pursuit of some goal, even if it is simply to get through the work day and go home to watch television. Your current station in life is a reflection of the quality of the goals you have set thus far, not a statement about your inherent potential. Anyone can change the quality of their life—at any time—by setting and pursuing more meaningful goals.

A compelling set of goals is not a luxury—something to pursue when it's most convenient—but rather a necessity. You will face adversity in your life, whether or not you have set worthy goals. By setting goals that inspire you, you develop a measure of strength that allows you to handle the obstacles that occur. If you do not set goals for yourself, no one else will, and the vacuum that exists will be filled with whatever comes along, often something negative. When you set a goal, you are saying, "This is what I want, and this is what I will have." You make no excuses. You set about your work, determined to reach your goal, no matter what.

How do you know if the goal you have chosen is the right one for you? How do you know if your goal is worthy of your efforts? Consider this: success for you will begin the moment you decide that you would rather fail at your greatest undertaking than continue to achieve at your current level. When the pursuit of a goal—regardless of whether you succeed or not—has more meaning to you than obtaining anything else, then you have chosen a worthy goal.

There is nothing in the world really beneficial that does not lie within the reach of an informed understanding and a well directed pursuit.

—EDMUND BURKE

Weak goals induce low expectations and moderate aspirations. Weak goals will not challenge you to work your hardest or perform at your best. Without a strong motivation, derived from worthy goals, the struggle to succeed against adversity can become insurmountable.

Goals chosen without passion will never deliver results worth owning. Why pursue meaningless goals that contain no real value for you? It is a mistake to pursue goals simply because you think you can accomplish them. The fact that you can find and hold a job is no reason to stay in that job, if what you really want is to start your own business or go back to school.

Without taking the time to set your goals, the journey to success can never begin. Only you know what it is you want; only you can set your goals. How far you pursue your goals is also up to you. You can go *all the way*; or stop after only partial attainment, if you believe you have received all of the benefits available. If you choose to abandon your goal, move on and immediately set a new goal.

Believe that your goals are attainable

Can you honestly say that you have spent all day, every day, thinking of and working toward your goal? Of course not; most people spend very little time examining and pursuing their goals. And most people are never as successful as they would like to be. Is this a coincidence, or a predictable pattern? Certainly, the more time and effort that you apply toward your goal, the more likely you are to get there.

You must have a realistic sense that you can achieve the goals you've set— otherwise you will end up chasing a vision that seems to keep moving further away. An elusive goal suggests one or all of the following:

• You don't have faith in your ability to achieve it.

• You are chasing a dream rather than a specific, tangible goal.

• You don't really want to reach your goal.

Belief in your goal as worthy and attainable creates the energy to achieve it. You must first come to believe that your goal *is* attainable. Next, you have to believe that you *can* achieve it. And last, you need to believe that you *will* reach it.

Your success in achieving your goals rests primarily with your level of desire for, belief in, and commitment to those goals. These attitudes have a direct impact on your day-today actions. When you believe in your goals, you work harder at achieving them. When you work harder, you achieve more, reinforcing your belief. Be sure you choose goals that you believe in, goals that you think yourself capable of achieving, then get to work. This process will never fail you.

ARTICULATE YOUR DREAM INTO A TANGIBLE GOAL

You can have anything you want—if you want it badly enough. You can be anything you want to be, have anything you desire, accomplish anything you set out to accomplish—if you will hold to that desire with singleness of purpose...

—ROBERT COLLIER

Set goals that create opportunities

Setting goals allows you to plan for the future and organize your activities so that you maximize your chances of obtaining your goals. What goal setting cannot do is *predict* the future. Through goal setting you can minimize the setbacks and failures that will occur, but you will never be able to account for every eventuality.

This is where your power of perseverance comes into play. Set interim goals that increase the probability of achieving your dream, rather than trying to guarantee the outcome. Look to increase your opportunities to succeed, and strengthen your resolve to never give up when inevitable adversities arise.

Working from goals encourages you to focus on the future by controlling the present, rather than looking to the past. It is only in today's actions that progress can be made. It's imperative that the goals and milestones you set for yourself reflect the daily opportunities that are available to you.

Most of us have attempted to set goals at some time in our lives, probably with mixed results. Striving for important goals and coming up short, again and again, can create a negative pattern of failure that can inhibit us from future attempts to succeed. However, past failures, regardless of their frequency, should never prevent us from setting new goals. In order to disrupt this cycle, set smaller, more achievable goals until you have regained the confidence necessary to attack a more difficult goal.

What specific steps will take you toward your goal? Begin them immediately. If you have not yet devised the necessary plan of action, start there; create a step-by-step plan that culminates in the realization of your goal.

Nothing will ever be attempted if all possible objections must be first overcome.
—SAMUEL JOHNSON

Great accomplishments begin with the desire to increase your reach, to improve your grasp. What lies in the distance can be yours as soon as you decide that you truly want it. Decide what it is that you want. Then make a plan and stick to it. Stop only when you have succeeded, and immediately choose and work toward your next goal.

Put your goals to words

Whatever we aspire to, we must put it to words. Define your goals clearly and put them in writing. Success has been defined as the pursuit of worthwhile goals. How, then, can you ever consider yourself successful if you have not set any goals? It is common to have a mental image of your goal, but never put it to paper and pen, never say it aloud. Writing down your goals will help you to define exactly what it is you want to achieve. Telling someone else about your goals reinforces your commitment to succeed.

We start with a dream that transcends our daily activities; a dream that pulls us, rather than pushes us, forward. It's important to set goals that satisfy our definition of personal fulfillment. In order to achieve the more significant desires that we harbor, it is vital that our goals be made up of dreams that are important to *us*, rather than simply being motivated by the need to please those around us. The ideal goals are those that are beneficial to ourselves as well to others. If you remain honest with yourself, and seek to pursue goals that are truly representative of your most important dreams and desires, your influence on those around you will be positive and enriching.

> *The difference between doers and dreamers is that the latter wait for the mood before taking action while the former create the mood by acting.*
> —Daniel Gerson

We all have a vision of what success might hold for us. The problem rests with the clarity of our vision. You must be able to define what success feels like, and what it looks like. Take some time to describe, in detail, what you want to become and to have, and how you are going to achieve it. Be specific. How does it look? Who is there? What are you doing?

Maintaining an awareness of what you want, where you are headed, and the manner in which you will get there provides you with the strength and courage you will need to sustain your focus and avoid distractions.

Taking action in the pursuit of our goals is easy—when we are in the right mood. The maintenance of our moods then becomes a primary area of focus. However, we must learn to continue with goal-related actions regardless of our mood. The more we behave in a manner consistent with our goals, the more our moods will reflect our goal-related desires.

Your goals should be challenging

The goals you set should be based on reality, not fantasy; otherwise you are setting yourself up for grief and frustration. Your goals should be challenging—if they aren't, they won't provide much energy or inspiration—but not unreachable. As a rule, your goals should have about a 50 percent chance of success. They should cause you to stretch, but not to break.

In *This Business of Writing*, author Gregg Levoy states that although "...it's important to acknowledge your limitations and be 'reasonable' in your expectations, it is equally vital to recognize that what any of us is capable of achieving is orders of magnitude beyond what conventional wisdom would indicate and probably what we ourselves think we can." We will never know just how good we are, or how good we can become, until we decide to find out.

When setting your initial goals, your inherent potential is very important in determining how successful you will be. For example, if you are capable of running 10 miles per week, you should set a higher goal than: "In one year I will be running 15 miles per week." At the same time, you should not try to double your mileage in the following week. A more reasonable goal for you would be to increase your mileage by 10 to 15 percent each week, with the ultimate goal to eventually run 25 miles per week. This is a significant and worthwhile goal, achievable in small, measured increments.

According to Gilbert Brim, a leading social scientist and author of *Ambition*, we should "...choose challenges that are difficult enough to perplex and test our powers yet not so tough that we are likely to face severe or frequent failure. Most of the time we try to arrange things so that we are neither pushed to the limit nor coasting, neither overloaded nor underloaded." We must create a cycle of achievement, full of opportunities for success.

Seek ye first the good things of the mind, and the rest will either be supplied or its loss will not be felt.
—FRANCIS BACON

Set goals that contain enough of a challenge to inspire you to go beyond any of your previous boundaries. When setting performance standards, it's okay to use your past performance as a gauge, but always try to use a multiplier; that is, try to perform at some percentage rate higher in the future. When setting goals, try not to under- or overestimate your abilities. The former creates boredom, the latter anxiety. Be honest with yourself about your abilities, and you will set goals that are challenging and attainable.

Inspirational writer Og Mandino, in *The Greatest Secret In The World*, explains how he improves his value through setting goals: "First I will set goals for the day, the week, the month, the year, and my life...so must I have objectives before my life will crystallize. In setting my goals I will consider my best performance of the past and multiply it a hundredfold. This will be the standard by which I will live in the future." Set progressive goals that allow for greater successes at each level.

There can be no success without progress

To succeed you must begin, improve, make adjustments, and keep going. As long as you are engaged in a project that holds meaning for you, your rate of progress is less important than just getting started. At first you will make mistakes, and progress will come in spurts. But resolve to begin anyway, for you cannot attain those things in life that you have not sought. You must start at the beginning of your goal and seek out daily progress and improvement.

Do what you can, with what you have, where you are.
—THEODORE ROOSEVELT

There can be no success without progress, and there can be no progress without a first step. A common mistake that many of us make is to give up on a goal before we have even begun. The realization of our goal seems so far off, and the work it will take to get there appears so overwhelming, that we become paralyzed with inactivity. This paralysis can keep our goal out of reach forever. The only way to counter this is to begin, to take the first step. Today. Now. There is nothing more powerful, nothing that can be more pressing, than taking the first step toward our success.

Many people get caught up endlessly trying to decide where or how to start. You must begin the process with action, any action, no matter how small. Make the first step an easy one; it will serve as the springboard for your next action, and its content is not nearly as important as its commencement.

Begin today. Don't hesitate, not even for a moment. Delays create anxiety, anxiety breeds inertia, and inertia requires tremendous energy to overcome. By not creating an inert situation in the first place, less energy is expended, thus saving your energy for the creative process.

Success is achieved in small steps

Rarely will one specific action result in a major accomplishment; rather, we build success with small, incremental steps, one upon another. In this way, after some period of time, major goals are achieved. It's unimportant what you choose as your first step, only that you remember to take the steps toward your goal, one at a time. If you add one block to another, eventually a building will stand. This is how all great things are built, tangible and intangible alike. Begin with a strong, solid foundation and move on from there.

Your success rests primarily with your ability to develop short-range, easy-to-achieve sub-goals that make up the larger goal. This is why it's important to create a series of short-term goals or milestones. Break down your goal so that each sub-goal takes you one step closer. Since these smaller goals are all we have control over, they contain all the power. Focus your energy on these smaller goals, and they will lead you to your ultimate success.

Try to schedule the steps leading to your goal to allow the accomplishment of one or more tasks each day. When you are able to make progress toward your goal on a daily basis, you will benefit from an increased sense of achievement. Every time you reach a milestone in the pursuit of your goal, you boost your confidence in your ability to succeed.

Rarely is a dream realized in a single day. Often it takes

years. Great outcomes are achieved through the accumulation of successful days, one added to another. A successful day consists of many successful moments joined together. Maintain an awareness of this principle as well as a definite mental image of your outcome. Stay aware of where you have been, where you are, and most importantly, where you want to go. If previous actions have not gotten us to where we want to be, then our methods must be examined and changed. We must constantly think about our next step, while also keeping an eye on our goal in the distance.

The drops of rain make a hole in the stone not by violence, but by oft falling.
—LUCRETIUS

Dr. Roberto Assagioli, the founder of Psychosynthesis, writes in *The Act of Will* that the only plans we have direct control over are "...the modest little goals; the trick of planning a successful life is to stack together these smaller goals in a way that increases your chances of reaching the long-range goals you really care about." Each day then should be treated as crucial to your success—each day's efforts, when added to the collected efforts of the previous days, will eventually lead to the successful attainment of your goal.

To achieve your goal you must start with step one, proceed to step two, and so on until you are finished. There are no shortcuts. Every step is significant, and each should be infused with the passion of your dream.

Consider the patience and endurance it takes to become an accomplished runner. A person beginning a running program cannot go out the first time and compete. You must first put in the miles, work on your form, increase your pace, and so on. As a runner, you can set many different goals such as distance or speed, but one constant is continuous, daily practice. You go from one level of fitness to the next; the laws of the physical world preclude skipping a level.

You will not be able to skip levels of progress in life any more than you can skip them when you are learning to run. You need to run four miles before you can progress to five. Similarly, you need to reach short-term goals before you can achieve your most coveted goal.

One cannot mount a camel that has not yet arrived, or one that has already departed.

—ORIENTAL MAXIM

If you find yourself getting off track, refocus on your goal and eliminate distractions, one by one. Be ruthless if you need to be. Examine the activities you routinely perform and do away with the ones that are not conducive to your success. Success depends entirely on your ability to stick with the tasks of your choosing, no matter how long it takes or how hard it becomes.

Steps in goal setting:

- *Decide exactly what it is you desire most, what dreams you want to achieve.* Without first selecting the appropriate outcome, most ventures are doomed to fail.

- *Articulate these desires and dreams into tangible, specific, positive goals.* We will always perform at a higher, more efficient level when aiming at a specific goal or outcome.

- *Choose realistic goals.* Try goals with about a 50 percent chance of success. Learn the difference between goals that are significant and goals that are based on self-delusion.

- *Set goals that are in your sphere of influence.* Trying to manipulate tasks that are out of your realm of control is frustrating and self-defeating.

- *Outline the steps you need to take to reach your goal.* Start with the last task that will have to be accomplished and then the next-to-last, and so on until you have arrived at a step that you can take today.

- *Set about accomplishing the first task, work at it until it is achieved, then move on to the next step.* The current task is all you have control over—finish it and be done with it.

- *Maintain a mental image of yourself as having attained your goal.* The more you imagine you have achieved it, the more intense the image becomes. This single step provides tremendous motivation.

- *Continue this process until you have succeeded in obtaining your goal, and then immediately set new goals.* Never rest on your accomplishments.

WITH PERSEVERANCE, MOST GOALS ARE ATTAINABLE

I hold to a doctrine, to which I owe not much, but all the little I ever had, namely, that with ordinary talent, and extraordinary perseverance, all things are attainable.

—Sir Thomas Fowell Buxton

Perseverance is essential to your success

Without a strong desire to persevere, your bigger goals will never be realized. Perseverance is essential to your success—more than talent, education, or money. You simply cannot maintain any degree of progress toward important goals without a concentrated effort applied in the right direction, combined with the ability to overcome the obstacles that arise.

You must work at maintaining your momentum when your resolve wanes. Keep your strength of perseverance close at hand and rely on it often, reaching for its power when you are faltering. The ability to give ourselves the gift of strength and endurance, of courage and commitment, of hope and honor; this is the power that perseverance gives us.

There will always be other people who have more talent, money, and advantages than you, but a firm strength of purpose gives you the opportunity to be the equal of anyone. The common denominator for all who achieve greatness is their ability to get through difficult passages, to maintain an unwavering resolve to succeed, until they reach their goal.

The attainment of any significant goal depends largely on

your ability to continue striving even when you want to quit with every fiber of your being. How willing you are to persevere in tough times is a telling indication of your chances of success. There is simply no other quality more important to accomplishing a great goal than perseverance. The ability to weather the storm of trial has delivered more people to their goals than has any other trait.

Author Ari Kiev, M.D., Clinical Associate Professor of Psychiatry at Cornell University Medical College, is a strong believer in the power of perseverance. He says perseverance "... will energize your desire to achieve, reduce your fear, and foster confidence in your ability. Perseverance gives a sense of limitless time, which permits you to persist until you reach your objective without rushing to finish, without perfectionistic inhibitions, and without cessation." He further states that through "...persistence and repeated small steps, continually moving toward your objective, you will eventually gain the power and expertise to reach it."

Meet setbacks with strength

The frequency with which you draw on your strength of perseverance depends on your goal, but the process is essentially the same for everyone. We encounter a setback or obstacle, and this point becomes a fork in the road. We can either choose to quit, and avoid the problem, or we can meet it head-on and persevere.

Peak performers always take the high road; they immediately attack their problem and seek to solve it, regardless of the resistance. When this pattern is repeated—when adversity is met with strength and commitment, time after time—we draw ever closer to our goal, gaining strength with each new victory.

Your level of achievement is directly influenced by your ability to maintain your progress despite the adversity you encounter. You are not born with either the ability to persevere or the inclination to quit; these are tendencies that have developed over a lifetime of experience. But you are not bound by your past; regardless of how many times you have backed down from challenges, you can at any time choose to become someone who perseveres, who never quits. Perseverance can be cultivated. Each time you see a problem through to its resolution, you will have new strength and wisdom to draw on for the next challenge.

Some problems that you encounter will be easily solved, and the effort will seem minimal. Perseverance becomes important only when all other devices at our disposal have failed us, when all we can do seems simply not enough to get us through. At these times you will have to draw on all of the commitment, faith, and desire that you have pledged to your goal, for this is where your strength resides. Without a strong commitment to your goals, belief in your abilities, and a desire for success, your plans will collapse at the first sign of trouble.

Be willing to apply the maximum effort

There are two endings to any pursuit: results or excuses. You either see your goal through to the end, or you quit and create excuses for your decision. If you persevere, you may not end up with exactly what you had hoped for; but remember that your goals and plans should be fluid and flexible—wherever you end up, it will be somewhere worthwhile. Having the will to endure, the determination to persist, and the courage to persevere all but guarantees your success. Likewise, lacking these qualities nearly ensures you of defeat and failure.

Secure in the knowledge that hard work will pay off, peak performers work tirelessly toward their goals, extending their comfort zones and testing their commitment. Without this fierce will to endure, nothing of significance can be obtained. You must be willing to apply the maximum effort, no matter how much resistance you encounter.

Austere perseverance, harsh and continuous, may be employed by the least of us and rarely fails of its purpose, for its silent power grows irreversibly greater with time.
—GOETHE

Winners reach their goals because they persevere to the end; they persevere because they believe that eventually their efforts will lead them to their dreams. They do the work and endure the hardship until they have achieved all that is important to them. People who don't succeed usually don't even begin to attempt the important tasks, and are seldom in a position to know what true perseverance requires. There is no great mystery to the methods that winners use; winners succeed simply because they persevere.

As hard as it may be, no quality is more important to goal achieving than perseverance. The ability to endure the work for just one more day will eventually, as the days add up, dramatically improve your chances of succeeding.

LEARN THE DIFFERENCE BETWEEN DIFFICULT AND IMPOSSIBLE

If your determination is fixed, I do not counsel you to despair. Few things are impossible to diligence and skill. Great works are performed not by strength, but by perseverance.

—SAMUEL JOHNSON

Goals are achieved through repeated efforts

Sustaining momentum while in the pursuit of lofty goals is not always easy, but while it may be difficult to work through the challenges that you face, it certainly isn't impossible. A worthy goal has not gotten hold of you until you begin doing the things that the average person considers impossible. High achievers understand that what most of us consider impossible is actually just difficult. We are all capable of great accomplishments, but lacking the confidence to do what seems difficult, we tend to set weak, modest goals, and never attempt to achieve our most coveted goals.

Often, overcoming adversity is simply a matter of placing things in their proper perspective. Adversity to one person is no more than a minor inconvenience to another. If others are obtaining the results you desire, there must be a way for you to gain these results as well. Winners know that with clear goals and perseverance, nothing is out of their reach.

How often have you given up on a goal because you felt you lacked the necessary talent? High achievers understand that talent is *not* synonymous with success. Success has more to do with your ability to do the work and stay with it, regardless of the obstacles you encounter, until you have reached your goal. It will always be the most persevering individuals—not simply the most talented—who consistently reach their goals.

Anyone of average ability who applies himself will achieve greater success than the more talented individual who expects excellence, yet does little to achieve it. Possessing great natural ability is not always an aid to success if the desire or motivation to succeed is not there. Lack of ambition, brought on by weak desire, will nullify any chance of long-term success. The greatest skills, when coupled with a negative attitude or a lack of effort, will always result in failure.

Courage and perseverance have a magical talisman, before which difficulties disappear and obstacles vanish into air.
—JOHN QUINCY ADAMS

Make the most of your time, energy, and abilities, and you will make huge gains toward your goals. Focus on what you *can* control and influence; do not squander your resources on tasks or activities that rest outside your sphere of control. By creating a plan that directs all of your actions toward your goal, your reactions and attitudes will be motivated by your success, and the results will follow.

More goals are obtained through repeated effort than by any other means, including high intelligence and extraordinary talent. Anyone of average or even modest talent can accomplish great feats by persevering, by staying with a project until it is complete. When you can hang on no matter how many times you meet with setbacks and disappointments, there is no limit to what you can learn, achieve, or become.

Achieving long-term goals is often compared to distance running. Both activities improve with practice and require time for tangible results to appear. Every step offers the opportunity, and the temptation, to quit. And both require simultaneous concentration on the destination and the next step. Successful distance runners know that their greatest asset is their stamina, their ability to endure just a few more miles, even when their body wants to quit.

In the ordinary business of life, industry can do anything which genius can do, and very many things which it cannot.
—HENRY WARD BEECHER

Maintain a positive attitude

Success demands that we create and take the ideal action, and that we maintain a positive, goal-oriented attitude. It is rarely dependent on the skills or talents with which we begin. Natural talent is inherited, but the development of talent comes only through effort. When you focus your thoughts and efforts on becoming successful, your abilities will naturally advance.

Little is impossible to those who focus, practice, and persevere in their endeavors. It is common to think that successful people were born with an aptitude for their work, but it is much more likely that they spent years developing and strengthening their skills. Most high achievers attribute their gains to the level of intensity applied to their efforts, rather than any innate natural abilities.

In his book, *Even Eagles Need a Push*, David McNally

discusses the value of natural talent versus a strong desire to achieve: "The *LA Times* published a report recently on a 5 year study of 120 of America's top artists, athletes, and scholars. Benjamin Bloon, A University of Chicago education professor who led the team of researchers, said, 'We expected to find tales of great natural gifts. We didn't find that at all. Their mothers often said it was their other child who had the greater gift.' The study concluded that the key element common to all of these successful people was, surprisingly, not talent but an extraordinary drive and determination."

The term *over-achiever* is often used to label people who consistently obtain results greater than their natural abilities would suggest is possible. A more precise term is *high achiever*—someone who pushes beyond the limits of his or her talent with persistence, hard work, and determination. Anyone can become a high achiever. It is equally important to understand what it means to be an *under-achiever*—those who tend to give up easily in the face of difficulty and who never live up to their potential. Our achievements are a reflection of our tenacity, rather than a measure of our talent.

> *The miracle or the power that elevates the few is to be found in their industry, application and perseverance under the prompting of a brave, determined spirit.*
>
> —MARK TWAIN

Stay with your goal as long as it takes

Making a commitment to persevere in the face of any and all obstacles that present themselves can make up for any shortcoming or deficiency that you perceive in yourself. Once you commit to never giving up, you gain a strength that can see you past any barrier. Staying with your goal as long as it takes is what will lead to its realization—no other tool is as important to goal attainment as perseverance.

Perseverance is an attribute that is learned over time, as you are tested by trial after trial, obstacle after obstacle. Only with experience can you develop the confidence required to see your ventures through. You will always gain strength through the concentration of your effort and the development of your endurance.

While it's important to spend time devising detailed plans that will lead you to your goal, unless you can put those plans into action—and fight back when they threaten to collapse—you will not succeed. Be prepared to make adjustments and sacrifices, and maintain an inner focus that keeps you always moving toward your goal.

CHAPTER 4

Making The Commitment

COMMITMENT DRIVES PERSEVERANCE

*There's a difference between interest and commitment.
When you're interested in doing something, you do it
only when it's convenient. When you're committed to
something, you accept no excuses, only results.*

—KENNETH BLANCHARD

Commitment is a sign of courage

If there exists any one secret to perseverance, it's
commitment. The achievement of any worthwhile goal
rests with your ability to become 100 percent committed to
that goal. Most experts in the field of motivation agree that
it is not the more gifted individuals who tend to excel, but
rather, those with the strongest commitment who seem to
consistently outperform their more talented counterparts.

Fortunately, those of us who aren't naturally gifted can compensate by developing a strong, focused commitment to our goals. This commitment, when coupled with an unswerving desire to persevere, can overcome almost any obstacle thrown our way.

Commitment is a sign of courage: the courage to discover what you really want and what it will take to get you there; the courage to make the correct decisions and then act on them; and the courage to impose your will on your environment so that you may succeed. Commitment begins with an awareness of your goals and a willingness to overcome or remove any obstacle that interferes with the realization of those goals. The depth of your commitment will influence the intensity of your efforts, and it is from your efforts that results will come.

[A winner is] a person who fulfills his contract with the world and with himself. That is, he sets out to do something, says he is committed to doing it, and in the long run does it.

—DR. ERIC BERNE

Stephen R. Covey, chairman of the Covey Leadership Center and the nonprofit Institute for Principle-Centered Leadership, describes two ways in which we can take immediate control of our lives: "We can *make a promise*—and keep it. Or we can *set a goal*—and work to achieve it." The inner integrity we begin to establish from making and keeping commitments, even small commitments, will provide us with the "...awareness of self-control and the courage and strength to accept more of the responsibility for our own lives. By making and keeping promises to ourselves and others, little by little, our honor becomes greater than our moods." By always keeping the promises we make, we also learn to moderate our desire to try and please everybody.

Your own veracity is the starting point for achieving your goals. Learn to make and keep commitments to yourself. Knowledge of what you can do, and of what you are willing to do, brings you power. Power helps you control the circumstances that affect you, and being in control of the outcome of the events in your life is a crucial step in becoming successful. If you cannot commit to your goal, you will lack the personal power necessary to bring about the attainment of that goal.

Commitment to an important and worthy goal, concentrated effort, careful planning, and perseverance are the cornerstones of any successful endeavor. If your goal is significant and your commitment is strong, all other devices necessary for your success will fall into place at the correct time. There is just no denying those who commit to a goal that transcends their daily lives.

Recommit yourself daily to your goal

You should only commit to a goal that is carefully chosen and that you believe is worthwhile. Commitment, coupled with a strong desire for success, makes much of the necessary work seem effortless. Plans write themselves. Results are easily obtained. Adversity is effortlessly overcome. But your commitment can wane, especially when results are not as quick to appear as you had hoped. To maintain the momentum you will need to finish, recommit yourself daily to your goal.

To persevere, you must possess an inspiring goal and an unyielding commitment to that goal. Clearly defining your goal and then committing to it will give you the strength and courage that is required to keep you going when you are most tempted to give up. Choose a goal, commit to its achievement and distance yourself from any other thoughts or action. Do this day after day and the results will follow.

Commitment may not always guarantee success, but the lack of it is certain to bring failure. For example, if you are committed to excelling in the game of baseball, you are always playing, attending games, and practicing to improve your game. No one has to make you do these things. The commitment you make to becoming a skilled baseball player is the driving force in your life. Without such a commitment, you cannot expect to become more than an average player. Peak performers possess a tremendous desire to be great at whatever they do. And it consumes them.

YOU ARE YOUR BIGGEST OBSTACLE

If you are distressed by anything external, the pain is not due to the thing itself, but to your estimate of it; and this you have the power to revoke at any moment.

—MARCUS AURELIUS

Expect obstacles to appear

If you were asked to name the single biggest obstacle that keeps most people from obtaining their goals, what would you say? Is it lack of money? Lack of time? Lack of motivation? While these are obstacles that many of us are familiar with, there is one that is far more powerful, and can be far more destructive—ourselves. Many of us have managed to unravel our most coveted goals through self-defeating behaviors. This does not mean that we don't want to be successful. It may simply indicate that we have not yet grasped the basic tools that we need to become successful. By making significant changes in two areas—our attitudes and our methods—we can remove ourselves as the biggest obstacle that lies in the path to our goals, and preserve our energy for overcoming the external problems that we cannot avoid.

In their book, *Leaders*, authors Warren Bennis and Burt Nanus discuss how successful leaders differ from others in their "...capacity to embrace positive goals, to pour one's energies into the task, not into looking behind and dredging up excuses for past events." Even those of us who have failed in past endeavors can become successful by changing our methods and developing a more positive attitude. Your attitude directly affects your behavior, and it is your behavior that determines your success in overcoming any obstacles you encounter. If we do not believe that we are worthy of our goal, or that our goal is worthy of the effort, then we will give up at the first sign of difficulty.

Expect obstacles to appear when you begin actively pursuing significant goals. You cannot control the occurrence of most of the adversity you will face, but you can control how you interpret and react to it. Don't ignore, hide from, or become angry with the problems you encounter; rather, focus your energy toward resolving them. If you reduce your problems to their smallest components and then work on finding the best solutions, one at a time, even the biggest obstacles can be overcome. Be prepared for the problems that will inevitably arise. Establish a consistent plan of action and rely on it when obstacles arise.

The superior man thinks always of virtue; the common man thinks of comfort.

—CONFUCIUS

Changing our attitudes and behaviors is not a simple task. Most of the internal resistance we feel is based on our experiences. Negative tension is created when we are steeped in memories of past failures and defeats. We express this tension through feelings of regret, disillusionment, and frustration, and we cannot be productive while in this state. Remember that past disappointments never have to equal future failures. You alone have chosen your path to this point, and you are now free to choose and pursue any new goal that you desire.

Don't dwell on what you cannot control

While we are not always in control of what may happen in our lives, we are *always* in control of our reactions to those events. No one is spared from disappointments or setbacks. But you must not let these events dictate your future. By meeting each obstacle head-on and drawing on all of your available resources, you can recover from any setback and maintain a positive, productive attitude no matter what befalls you.

Our grand business in life is not to see what lies dimly at a distance, but to do what lies clearly at hand.

—THOMAS CARLYLE

Many people overreact to the daily events that are beyond their control. If you find yourself spending a great deal of emotional energy worrying about people, places, or things that you cannot control or avoid, you need to put them in their proper perspective with respect to the important goals in your life. Don't allow daily hassles like traffic congestion or hostile people to drain you of the energy you need to pursue your goals. If these events lack any material impact on your life, and if you are unable to avoid them, then dismiss them from your thoughts. It is that simple.

If we want to be successful, why do we create so many obstacles for ourselves? These problems usually result from the constant, internal struggle that is waged between our intellect, which knows what we are supposed to be doing, and our emotions, which dictate what we want to be doing.

Author Robert Ringer describes this struggle when he says that "...[mastering] yourself is not the easiest of tasks, because within each of us exists a perpetual struggle between our intellect and our emotions." His solution for solving this struggle? Success through self-discipline, by "... acting on your intellectual conclusions and overriding your instinctive desire for instant gratification." Only you can decide to start acting in your best interest, and you can make this choice at any time.

Replace negative habits with productive ones

Self-discipline is something that is readily achieved, but not so easily maintained. That is, even though we are able to resist a temptation for the sake of our long-term goals in one instance, there is no assurance that we will be able to resist the next time. The only way to resolve this struggle is to change our behaviors, so that our short-term desires are in line with our long-term goals. We often encounter massive resistance when we try to change, but if we can replace negative habits with productive ones that fuel our success, we will win our most difficult battles.

When our actions are bringing us positive results, clearly we should continue those actions. Likewise, when our efforts do not bring positive results, we should discard those actions. Sometimes, though, even when our behavior is unproductive or even counterproductive, we have trouble letting go. The reasons that we allow unhealthy emotional attachments, negative habits, and addictions to continue to stand in the way of our success are personal and varied, but we must seek to understand why we are acting against our best interests.

We must identify our self-defeating behavior, so we can correct it and continue in a more productive direction. If we project the consequences of our everyday actions into the future, we are more likely to act in a manner consistent with our goals. One way to do this is to ask, "will this behavior or activity move me closer to or further away from my goal?"

Once you have examined your own resistance, and are sure that your habits are productive and your attitude is positive and goal-oriented, you must get on with the work at hand. Worrying about the future or regretting the past keeps us from putting forth the effort we need today to advance in the direction of our goals. We must remain confident, knowing that if our attitude is positive and our methods are sound, the intensity of our efforts will be reflected in the quality of our results.

The conditions of conquest are always easy. We have but to toil awhile, endure awhile, believe always, and never turn back.

—SIMMS

Commitment fuels your efforts

While our accomplishments teach us what we can achieve, our failure to reach a particular goal implies only that we have not yet arrived. It does not indicate that we will never achieve this goal. Concentrate on making things happen. You have absolute control over the results that you will or will not obtain, as well as control over your reactions to the obstacles you encounter.

Goals that continue to elude you may not hold sufficient importance in your life. When you find yourself losing interest in your goals, examine them to be sure you are still committed to their attainment. Only from commitment will come the energy to pursue your goals with the intensity they demand.

Once you are totally committed to a course of action, your energy becomes boundless. Your degree of energy is usually based on your psychological state; rarely is listlessness a result of any physical deficiency. If you cannot find the energy to complete the tasks at hand, you need to refocus, recommit, and increase your efforts. Commit yourself to your goals and to immediate action.

TRUST AND BELIEVE IN YOURSELF

Act as if it were impossible to fail.

—DOROTHEA BRANDE

As long as we have faith, we have hope

All progress is rooted in faith. Let your faith in yourself and in your goals be the cornerstone on which you build your successes. No great dream was ever realized without an unswerving belief in the value of that dream. No great obstacles were ever overcome without faith that the struggle would be rewarded. Count your faith as among the most valuable tools you bring to your efforts, greater than money, time, or talent. You can accomplish great things if only you believe you can.

You must begin your journey with an unshakable faith in yourself and in your dreams. Those who believe in themselves and their goals are always moving forward, seeking solutions, and focusing on their goals. As long as we have faith, we will have hope, and as long as we have hope, we can remain productive and resourceful. Successful solutions to the problems we encounter are only obtained in a productive and resourceful state of mind.

Those who have achieved a significant level of personal success will tell you that they went through periods of intense mental and physical trepidation, when all that sustained them was their belief in themselves and their goals. You must have this faith if you are going to succeed by persevering against the odds; from faith will come strength, resolve, and patience. Few things are impossible when your faith cannot be shaken.

Faith is not something that can be taught. It must come from a belief that you are worthy of the goals to which you aspire. High achievers accept and believe, without reservation, that they are destined to be successful.

If you believe in yourself and in the worthiness of your goals, all of your days can be good days. When faith is present, it works like magic. All problems seem small. Difficulties slide off you like water. Questions are posed and answers are provided. Work is applied and results follow. Alliances are forged and reinforced. Creations are original and forthcoming. Nothing is held back.

Good thoughts and actions can never produce bad results; bad thoughts and actions can never produce good results.

—JAMES ALLEN

There will be times when maintaining your faith seems effortless; undoubtedly, these are the times when things are running smoothly, when the work seems easy. But the depth of your faith will eventually be tested by adversity. While it will be your perseverance that will get you past the obstacles, it is your belief in your ability to persevere that will be the fuel for your endurance. Anyone who has struggled through adversity and setbacks can attest to the value of faith. Each time you draw on your faith to guide you through trouble, your faith will be strengthened. Faith gives our struggles a purpose—the purpose to renew our resolve and propel us forward toward our goals.

It doesn't matter from where you draw your faith, but if you don't believe in your goal, and if you don't believe that you can accomplish it, you will not succeed. When people give up on their dreams, it is often because they simply don't believe that they can accomplish what they envision. It is not a lack of money, time, or ideas that halts their progress; more often, it is a lack of faith. If you believe in it, you can achieve it. Miracles happen with faith. Develop your faith by practice, and it will be a powerful asset.

Expectations of success will bring success

Psychologists tell us that success raises our expectations and failure lowers them. The question to ask ourselves is, are we creating a climate of lowered expectations by imagining failure prior to an event? Of course! Likewise, we can create success by mentally raising our expectations. It works both ways. Expectations of success will bring success, just as expectations of failure carry the seed of failure. Losers never expect to win, and are seldom disappointed. Low expectations are a barrier through which we cannot progress.

You can make errors in almost any area of your life and still reach a high level of success if you only remember and apply this one thought: what you think about, what ideas you hold in your mind will, in time, manifest themselves in your life.

Everything that exists in your life right now is, at some emotional or intellectual level, what you have expected for yourself. If you are not happy with where you are today, raise your expectations so that you may aspire to them. By maintaining an attitude of high self-expectation and always keeping a vivid mental image of yourself succeeding—of being in possession of your goal—you will develop the strength of purpose that is vital to your ability to persevere during tough times.

You are not likely to meet many highly successful cynics. Almost to a person, high achievers are optimists. People who are expecting successful results tend to achieve successful outcomes. They maintain an ideal mental image of the result because they believe that their success, no matter how grand, is entirely within reach.

> *The thing always happens that you really believe in; and the belief in a thing makes it happen.*
> —FRANK LLOYD WRIGHT

How you view the results that you obtain along the way will determine what degree of success you will have. If you react negatively to your results—for example, if your progress is slower than you had hoped, and you conclude, "I will never get there"—your belief in your ability to succeed will suffer, and you are likely to quit. On the other hand, if you look for positive aspects of any result you obtain, no matter how small, you will be encouraged to continue. How you choose to view your progress is entirely up to you, and the results you obtain are under your control.

Direct all of your actions toward the accomplishment of your expectations. Begin by believing you can—and will—have it your way. Always expect to succeed. Imagine it; practice it, again and again. Become preoccupied with success.

Make the decision to always move forward, to trust in your instincts, and trust in yourself. Have faith in your ability to achieve the greatness that you imagine. The moment you begin to believe—really believe—that you are in charge of your life—that your desire, perseverance, and courage will dictate your ultimate results—this is when you will begin to experience true success.

Nothing worthwhile was ever achieved without overcoming numerous bouts of adversity. Again and again, our will to continue is tested by external as well as internal challenges. We must be prepared to face these obstacles; our commitment to our goal and our desire to see it through must outweigh the temptation to quit.

MAKING THE CORRECT CHOICE

If we don't change our direction, we're likely
to end up where we're headed.

—CHINESE PROVERB

Success depends on making correct choices

The choices you make right now, no matter how insignificant they seem, will determine your direction. Every choice you make suggests an effort and an action on your part. Your success depends on making the correct choice every time that you are faced with a decision. You must decide that you want to be successful and make decisions that will lead you down that path.

If you are willing to take the positive action necessary to achieve your goals, you will be successful. You are *who* you are, *what* you are, and *where* you are because of the *choices* you have made and continue to make. Everything that you have in your life today is there because you have chosen it, and you will continue to receive those things until you begin to make new choices.

Be aware of every choice you make, every day, and be sure that it is in accord with your goal. By controlling the present, everything else will fall into place. It is in the present moment, with the choices we make, that we will or will not become what we have resolved to become.

There is nothing so fleeting and undefinable as the present moment; once you allow a moment to pass, you have lost the chance to act. It's important to make choices with wisdom and confidence as opportunities present themselves.

Too many of us act as though we have an unlimited amount of these moments. We may wake up one morning and realize that the opportunities to act are gone and our goals are forever out of reach.

When we are inactive, we witness one precious moment after another pass us by. Practiced inertia breeds laziness, reinforcing our bad habits and compounding our lack of progress. The best way to break this cycle is to become so focused on your goal that all of your choices are made with the intent of reaching your goal.

Learn to distinguish between what is truly important and what is unnecessary. By always making the most productive choice, instead of the most desirable or impulsive choice, each moment, every day, you will achieve success. The ideal environment in which to operate exists when the things you desire are in harmony with the tasks that make up your goal.

> *Wisdom is knowing what to do next, skill is knowing how to do it, and virtue is doing it.*
> —David Starr Jordan

Identify each key decision point as it occurs. Use only truth and reality as your guide; do not allow your emotions to force you to make irrational decisions. If you consistently make positive, goal-oriented decisions, you will eventually reach your goal.

Every choice is a turning point

In *Getting Unstuck*, professor Sidney B. Simon suggests that every time you make the attempt to change, you encounter "...many moments of truth...moments when you act upon your choices or do not act, when you move forward or turn back, when you take a step or postpone it." We are faced with many choices, and each choice is a turning point. Simon concludes, "If you exercise your will and mobilize energy, all the work you did to clear other obstacles from your path will pay off, and you will truly be on your way to the life you desire and deserve."

To succeed, you must persist in your efforts daily. Each time you make a choice that relates to your goal, you draw closer to its realization. There will be times when you will make the wrong choice—the journey to success is never a straight, unobstructed road—but you will always have the opportunity to get back on track if you stray. Never allow the fear of choosing the wrong direction keep you from making a decision.

Base every choice you make on a plan that will lead you to your goal. Make every decision with your ultimate success in mind. Concentrating on the choices you make:

- Allows you the chance to examine your past actions and how they have shaped your current situation.

- Gives you the opportunity to change your present behavior.

- Provides the environment to effect a change on your future.

While making careful choices is important, it's not enough; each choice suggests an action that must be taken. Having the courage to *pull the trigger* is just as important as choosing where to direct your efforts. More people fail at this point— the point of action—than any other. But if you persevere, and proceed, you will notice that the choices become easier, and new opportunities arise that otherwise would have been absent. Make a habit of always making the correct choice, and you will be rewarded with great results. From results, you will gain progress; progress will lead to experience, and from experience will come the achievement of your goals.

PAYING THE PRICE OF SUCCESS

That which we obtain too easily, we esteem too lightly. It is dearness only which gives everything its value. Heaven knows how to put a proper price on its goods.

—THOMAS PAINE

There are no shortcuts

Nothing great is ever accomplished without sacrifice. We always pay a price for our endeavors, whether it be the price of our success, or the price of our failure. Once we chose our goal, we cannot turn back; we must either make the sacrifices that success demands, or suffer the regret of never reaching our dreams.

The price of success often involves making difficult choices. We can choose to give up something now—like a time-consuming habit or an expensive luxury—so that we might obtain something of greater value later. Each time we are presented with the opportunity to sacrifice something for the good of our greater goal, we must recognize it as an opportunity to contribute toward our eventual success. When you engage in this type of thinking, giving up some unnecessary expenses or a few nights out with our friends hardly seems like sacrifice.

Remember that there are no shortcuts. To succeed, we must be thoroughly committed to achieving our goals. Success is not a part-time activity. Dedicate your life to the pursuit of your goals, and you will be rewarded with a quality of life far superior to anything you have ever experienced.

We can have anything we want, become anything that we imagine, if we are willing to pay the necessary price. Success can be costly; it might require us to endure periods of struggle, solitude, and sacrifice. We will have to give up those things that give us instant gratification, or that use time that could be better spent working toward our goals. Decide in advance what you are willing to go without in order to obtain your goals, and resolve not to regret the loss of these things. The results you achieve are always much greater than the sacrifices you make. But you must first make the sacrifices.

Regret for the things we did can be tempered by time;it is regret for the things we did not do that is inconsolable.
—SYDNEY J. HARRIS

What is the price of success? B.C. Forbes said, "The only caste in America is merit. A price has to be paid for success. Almost invariably those who have reached the summits worked harder and longer, studied and planned more assiduously, practiced more self-denial, overcome more difficulties than those of us who have not risen so far." All of us dream of success. Defining what it means to us begins the process of goal attainment; determining what price we must pay takes us to the next level. There are few people willing to put in the work and sacrifice required, day after day, to ensure the achievement of their dreams.

All barriers can be overcome

Remember that failure is simply the unwillingness or inability to do what is necessary to attain your goals. If you want to keep chasing your dream, you need only to decide to keep after it. As long as you do not quit, you haven't failed. Almost all barriers can be overcome, provided your desire to succeed is strong enough, and remains strong through all adversity.

Unsuccessful people tend to avoid direct confrontations with their problems. Avoidance and denial behaviors keep them from having to make any kind of decision with respect to the challenges that confront them. By avoiding the hard choices that might lead to success, they ultimately suffer more, by creating an environment of frustration, disappointment, and regret.

The most common types of avoidance behavior include procrastination, tentative or weak goal selection, and vague plans of action. These behaviors have obvious results; procrastination breeds inactivity, uncertain goals offer little or no motivation, and constant changes in direction leads us in circles. Each of these behaviors must be identified and eliminated.

Why do normally productive and sensible people sometimes act in ways that are detrimental to their success? Most of us are guilty of self-defeating behavior at one time or another. There are many theories as to why we engage in this self-sabotage: we may suffer from low self-esteem, fear of success, or an inability to commit. The origin of your behavior is unimportant. Identify your self-destructive habits, and resolve immediately to change.

High achievers are effective in meeting the great challenges that create great results. Success takes hard work to achieve and even harder work to maintain. But it will always be worth the effort. Armed with a goal and a plan, we know what we have to do. The only decision left is whether we are willing to make the sacrifices, do the work, and persevere until our success is assured.

A strong resolve is essential to your success

A strong resolve leads to a positive and focused mental attitude. It's when we feel the most discouraged and overwhelmed by life's challenges that we tend to make counterproductive decisions that steer us further from our goals. During difficult times, refocus your efforts toward strengthening your resolve to achieve your goals.

It's clear why so few of us display a strong resolve. It's just too easy to quit and move on to other ventures. But this is the precise pattern that we have to break. Other projects will always appear more lucrative and less risky, but if we continue to change directions, we will never achieve anything of significance. Significant goals take so long to achieve and the path is so laden with obstacles that anyone who approaches them with less than complete commitment will never succeed.

Any accomplishment requires effort, courage, and will; some goals involve more difficulty, others less. If we really go for what we want, we encounter one kind of difficulty; if we give up, we confront another.

—DAN MILLMAN

Those who operate in a state of total resolve understand that there will be setbacks, disappointments, and even temporary defeat. Resolve has been defined as *great determination*. Through our resolve we find the strength to push through setbacks, to maintain a positive outlook when facing disappointment, and most importantly, to start again when overcome by temporary defeat, regardless of how often we find ourselves picking up the pieces. *All* defeats are temporary when you possess great powers of resolve.

Despite your good intentions, without a fundamental character foundation from which to operate, the adversity you encounter will always overwhelm you. The strength that you draw from within is your greatest ally, and will keep you from giving up when external influences are tempting you elsewhere. Always strive for a focused, unrelenting determination that keeps you moving in the direction of your goals.

ENJOYING THE PURSUIT

*Throw away, in the first place, all ambition beyond that of
doing the day's work well. Find your way into work in
which there is an enjoyment of it and all shadows of
annoyance seem to flee away. Let each day's work absorb
your energy and satisfy your wildest ambition.*

—Sir William Osler

Your reward is the journey

There is no greater feeling of confidence than what we
experience when we are pursuing an important goal.
It is the *journey*—not the destination—that provides us with
the greatest sense of satisfaction. Success requires only that
you be in pursuit of a worthwhile goal; it will always be
your efforts that will bring you the most joy, rather than
the results.

The pursuit of your goals is the pinnacle of living. By striving to accomplish your goal—despite any adversity you
face along the way—you are living a life most people only
dream about. Your greatest rewards lie in the application
of effort, not in the short-lived excitement of reaching your
goals. It is far more fulfilling to have goals and to work
toward them than it is to actually attain them.

What you become while working toward your goals is more
important than the actual attainment of those goals. The
skills you acquire, the character you develop—these are the
things that count most in life. The defeat of adversity, along
with the conquest of fear, will bring with it a confidence
and a strength of character that carries over into all areas of
your life. It is unimportant what your goals are, so long as

they are worthy of your efforts and you are always in pursuit of them. When fully engaged in the pursuit of your goals the following occurs:

- *Your attention is focused exclusively on your task.* Your efforts are so concentrated that you may lose your sense of time. High achievers possess an acutely developed sense of focus and concentration that is central to their success.

- *You are in control of your actions and reactions.* When you stop worrying about your results and whether you are going to succeed or not, this is when you will be able to summon the effort required to get the job done.

- *You develop a high level of competence.* With practice comes skill; by repeated efforts in the same area, you begin to develop an uncommon command of your work.

- *Your personal problems begin to evaporate.* You become so immersed in your work that all other considerations are secondary. You make positive, goal-oriented choices that enhance all areas of your life.

Build upon your successes

Become ruthless in the pursuit of your goals. Approach all you do with an effort unequaled in your past activities. Build upon your successes, strive for results, and leave no doubts about your motives. Success is achieved by constant movement toward a meaningful and significant goal.

Start each day fresh, without allowing the prior days' struggles to diffuse your efforts. Spending too much time and energy dwelling on the past or worrying about the future can rob your current efforts of their effectiveness. Focus on the daily tasks that need completion and let the results take care of themselves.

Making daily progress toward your goals puts you in a class with winners and high achievers. By honoring your commitment to achieve your goals, you will become so consumed with the desire to succeed that nothing can hold you back.

By committing to a goal, you are in effect saying that you will succeed in obtaining your goal, no matter what, whatever it may be and whatever it takes. Back up this mental commitment with physical effort and resolve to do whatever is necessary, no matter how hard the work is or how long it takes. You must resolve to never give up and never give in. Your resolve will be evident by your success.

FALL DOWN SEVEN TIMES, STAND UP EIGHT

Even if he fails again and again to accomplish his purpose...the strength of character gained will be the measure of his true success, and this will form a new starting point for future power and triumph.

—JAMES ALLEN

Perseverance is the will to succeed

True perseverance results from a heartfelt commitment to reach your goal at any cost. Perseverance is being tenacious to the end; it is the will to accomplish your goal despite the odds against you, no matter how long or how difficult the struggle. Any goal of substance will require time and effort to see it through. By persevering long enough, you will certainly succeed. There are no shortcuts, no alternate routes. The work must be done, obstacles will appear, and your ability to persevere is among the most important assets at your disposal.

Do not confuse perseverance with stubbornness. Perseverance involves persisting through adversity toward a worthwhile predetermined goal, while stubbornness is an unreasonable defiance that is rarely based on any significant goal. Perseverance comes from the knowledge that we can and will succeed. The ability to remain working toward a goal long after others have quit is the signature of all high achievers. There is simply no other way to achieve our goals than through determined, persistent effort, through all adversity and setbacks.

Our past failures should never prevent us from pursuing our present goals. The number of times you have come up short in the past, even in pursuit of the same goal, has no material impact on what you choose to pursue today. What matters most is the commitment and energy that you bring to your current efforts; at any time, you can choose to become more self-disciplined and persevering, regardless of your past false starts and defeats. Successful people use the setbacks of the past to strengthen their resolve and renew their commitment to their current goals.

Anyone who has watched an infant learn to walk can understand the value of perseverance. How long should we allow a child to learn to walk? As long as it takes! Children don't stop trying to walk when they fall down, or because it's difficult. Most children eventually learn to walk, and the longer they persevere, the better they become. Approach every goal with the same determination. It will take as long as it takes, and if we are determined to never give up, we will eventually prevail.

What we do best or most perfectly is what we have most thoroughly learned by the longest practice, and at length it falls from us without our notice, as a leaf from a tree.

—THOREAU

Each time you work through an obstacle, no matter how tough, you dramatically increase your chances of succeeding. Continuing to move forward in spite of repeated setbacks provides you with a sense of power that you can draw on for the next challenge, and the next, and so on, until persevering becomes almost effortless as you draw closer to your goal. Resolve to persevere, no matter how many times you fall. Many successful efforts were built on the belief that if you try long enough and hard enough, you will succeed.

CHAPTER 5

Developing Your Personal Power

CREATING EXCELLENCE

We are what we repeatedly do. Excellence, then, is not an act, but a habit.

—ARISTOTLE

Develop your skills for success

No one can provide you with a blueprint for success that involves little or no participation on your part. Each time we are faced with a moment of truth—an opportunity to grow or to regress—we must look to our personal power to help us determine the ideal action, and then take it. In order to combat the fears, frustrations, and doubts that plague us when we pursue significant goals, we must develop and enhance a specific set of skills and attitudes that are fundamental to our success.

There is little that is impossible to achieve if:

- Your goal is carefully chosen.
- You fully commit to your goal.
- You develop the personal power you will need to reach your goal.
- You create and maintain an environment that is conducive to goal attainment.
- You persevere until you have succeeded.

The key to your success rests with your ability to make the most of your talents and to overcome the adversity that will inevitably block your path. Your aim should not be to experience an easy life, but rather, to develop the personal power that allows you to handle life on your terms, and to succeed in spite of adversity.

Pursue excellence, not perfection

The pursuit of perfection, while admirable, is pointless. Our goals will never be realized in their perfect form. Since our goals and plans are fluid, not static, they will always be evolving. When you set perfection as your goal, you are inviting failure. Perfection is an abstract state that is never achieved, and its pursuit will only bring frustration, defeat, and disappointment.

A far better goal is the pursuit of excellence. Excellence is an outcome that can be quantified, pursued, and eventually achieved. How good should you attempt to become? You should try today to surpass yesterday's results, and tomorrow should redefine today's efforts.

You carry with you a sense of how well you are doing in any particular venture. You know intuitively how you are performing. It is this self-awareness that provides much of the feedback you need to refine your actions and improve your efforts.

One way to make immediate gains in your self-confidence and the results you obtain is to finish everything you start. Make this the most important habit you develop. By always finishing the tasks that you begin, you will have less unfinished business lying around waiting to turn into obstacles, you will improve your output many times over, and you will become more selective in the projects that you choose.

I attribute my success to always requiring myself to do my level best, if only driving a tack straight.
—RUSSELL CONWELL

While your overall goal should be the pursuit of excellence, you will need to set precise interim goals to satisfy this. At what do you wish to excel? Your goal must be tangible, worthwhile, and attainable. When you first set out, look only for improvement; you should seek small, progressive steps toward your goal. Add each day's accomplishments to the next. By applying the maximum effort day after day, you will soon be rewarded with excellence in your endeavors.

Practice always brings improvement

Improvement comes only with practice and effort. Practice offers us the chance to be the equal of anyone, in any field. Working on our skills will enhance performance, provide us with confidence, and lead us in the direction of our goals. This principle applies to all activities and will never fail you. No matter how difficult the task, by working at it and continuing to practice, you will, in time, become better. And if you practice often enough, you will eventually become excellent.

In her book, *Long Quiet Highway*, Natalie Goldberg describes how she learned about practice through writing: "I loved writing enough to be willing to work at it, whatever emotional space I was in. Something became more important than my individual mood. Practice sustained me, rooted me. It gave me an unwavering foundation." She found something she could pursue, something at which she could excel, and it consumed her, allowing her to practice, improve, and reach for greatness.

> *Success in the long run depends on endurance and perseverance. All things come to him who has learned to labor and wait, whose talents develop in the still and quiet years of unselfish work.*
>
> —SIR WILLIAM OSLER

If you concentrate on your efforts, the results always follow. Any worthwhile endeavor, when worked on tenaciously, will yield results. With practice comes improvement, and with massive practice comes massive improvement. Working at even the most mundane daily tasks will help you develop a sense of discipline and character that is common to all high achievers.

Practice improves performance, period. Improved performance provides you with a sense of confidence that you would not otherwise have. Armed with this new confidence, you will practice harder and more often, creating a cycle of success that will propel you forward toward your goal. You can only learn by becoming a participant in the game.

Dr. Sidney B. Simon, in his book *Getting Unstuck,* shares his thoughts on the value of practice: "If you doubt you have the will to change, practice proves otherwise. If will has eluded you in the past and left you feeling like a failure, practice lets you rediscover success, build confidence, and identify your personal trouble spots so you can overcome them." Those times when your work is fueled by inspiration and creativity will come infrequently; you must seize those moments when they occur.

BREAKING OUT OF YOUR COMFORT ZONE

*If we accept the challenge of doing something—
anything—that breaks through our imagined limits, we
are less likely to accept these limits in the future. One step
up the ladder of courage tends to encourage another...*

—DAN MILLMAN

Comfort zones create boundaries

Our habits are our strength—*and* our weakness. Habits shape our personalities, and allow us to develop routines that give our daily lives the predictability that we need. Yet these same habits create a restrictive comfort zone, an area of safety and familiarity that is resistant to change, risk, and growth.

A comfort zone is an abstract and subjective realm of performance in which we comfortably operate. We tend to perform adequately while on sure and familiar footing, but we stumble when forced to extend beyond our perceived limits. The uncertainty of the future can keep us bound in our existing comfort zones indefinitely. Fear of the unknown can be a very powerful deterrent, but without risk, there will be no growth, and no great achievement.

Most of our actions are based on either our desire to embrace risk and grow, or to avoid potential pain and seek comfort. In *Life 101*, authors John-Roger and Peter McWilliams believe that what we have is "...based upon moment-to-moment choices of what we *do*. In each of those moments, we choose. We either take a risk and move toward what we want, or we play it safe and choose comfort." Making the "comfort choice" too often diminishes our opportunities. The fewer opportunities we have, the more likely we are to lead a life of safe and comfortable mediocrity.

Comfort zones create boundaries in our behavior that prevent us from attempting things outside the limits of those boundaries. We draw a line over which we will not venture. Most of us tend to limit ourselves more than we challenge ourselves. Each time we give in to the boundaries we have set, it becomes that much harder to break free of them. The motivation for staying within our boundaries is to reduce our potential for pain and disappointment, but in the process we also derail our chances for success and fulfillment.

Take the risks that success demands

If you aren't experiencing regular setbacks, you probably aren't extending to the full range of your potential. The presence of problems and setbacks suggests that you are operating at the edge of your comfort zone, expanding your range and quality of effort. Similarly, the absence of adversity suggests the lack of a challenge. Until you start taking risks that stretch the boundaries of your comfort zone, success will elude you.

Your objective then is to expand your comfort zone, to take the risks that success demands. This may involve a complete overhaul of your habits, or simply altering them enough to allow you room to pursue your goals with the energy and resources that they require. Be willing to have an expansive comfort zone, one that allows you to form new, productive habits that contribute to your goals.

Dr. Willie Unsoeld, the first American to climb Mt. Everest, said this about breaking out of our comfort zones: "You need an element of risk, a challenge to perform at your peak. The right amount of risk throws you into a state of total concentration where there is nothing but the moment. You feel as if you have more time and more strength to accomplish things than you ever thought possible." The *right* amount of risk is the key. Too much of a risk can lead to disaster, while too little risk suggests complacency.

> *The law of worthy life is fundamentally the law of strife. It is only through labor and painful effort, by grim energy and resolute courage, that we move on to better things.*
>
> —THEODORE ROOSEVELT

We all operate in different comfort zones in our physical, social, and professional arenas. You may have a more expansive physical comfort zone than social; for example, when you are exercising, you feel confident and self-assured. You are not afraid to push your body to the limits of its potential, because you are sure of the rewards. But in social situations, you become shy and awkward, afraid to reach out and meet someone new. An examination of our various comfort zones will lead to interesting insights.

Consider also that a restrictive comfort zone to one person is an expansive comfort zone to another. Too often we compare our efforts and our results with others, and our perceived deficiencies frustrate us. The only boundaries that you should be concerned with are your own—your personal growth and achievement should never be measured by another's standards. Never allow yourself to be defined by anyone else.

Suffering is always optional

Each time you step out of your comfort zone you will experience some discomfort; this is necessary if you are to grow, and growth is necessary if you are to achieve your goals. While it is inevitable that we experience some growing pains, it is not necessary to suffer from this discomfort. Suffering is always optional—embrace discomfort as a sign of growth and progress.

You want to create a comfort zone that is expansive rather than restrictive, where you are best poised to strike when opportunities arise, and where your efforts can produce maximum results. Operating below this level for any length of time leads to lowered expectations, and your results will suffer.

One can choose to go back toward safety or forward toward growth. Growth must be chosen again and again; fear must be overcome again and again.
—ABRAHAM MASLOW

Maintain a clear, focused mental image of your ideal outcome. Do not be afraid to stray from your comfort zone when the extra effort is required. Once we achieve our goal, we must immediately set a new goal, at a higher level of difficulty, so that our comfort zones are constantly expanding. While our initial efforts may have seemed difficult and demanding, as we reset our goals and our boundaries, our definition of difficult also will change.

Breaking out of our comfort zone requires a concentration of faith and effort, as well as a certain measure of sacrifice and discomfort. By remaining in a restrictive comfort zone for all or most of our lives, we produce results well below our potential, leaving our goals unfulfilled. Either way, whether we take risks and extend ourselves, or choose to play it safe, our lives are difficult. Taking risks, however, provides us with hope, potential for growth, and the opportunity to achieve our goals. Armed with the knowledge that all things are possible with faith, effort, and perseverance, we must choose to step out of our self-imposed boundaries and into the arena of risk and challenge, for therein lies the fulfillment of our dreams.

FOCUS ON TODAY

*We can easily manage if we will only take each day, the
burden appointed for it. But the load will be too heavy for
us if we carry yesterday's burden over again today and
then add the burden of the tomorrow to the weight before
we are required to bear it.*

—JOHN NEWTON

Today's actions will determine your success

Your success hinges only on today's actions. Dwelling
on the past, on why you did this or failed to do that,
often leads to regret and depression. At the same time,
excessive concern for the future can breed high levels of
anxiety, leaving you paralyzed with fear and doubt. It is
only the actions of the present that will determine if your
future will bring you achievement and success or
disappointment and failure.

Living in the present is the single greatest gift available to
us. This does not imply that we should pursue instant gratification; it means we should enjoy where we are today,
doing all we can to improve our lot for tomorrow. When
tomorrow arrives, it will be that much more enjoyable because of yesterday's actions.

How do we live in the present? We set worthwhile goals,
commit to those goals, develop our personal power, and
create an environment that allows us to pursue our goals
to the utmost of our abilities. We leave yesterday's problems behind and work only on today. We look ahead to the
possibilities of the future, but live firmly in the present.

When you aren't preoccupied with the past, or worried about the future, you will be able to concentrate better on the present. Concentrate on today's tasks, and how you will accomplish them. What is it that lies before you to do this day? Use the past only as a source of knowledge and information, as a way to learn from your mistakes so as not to repeat them. Do what is in front of you and then move on to the next step. Resolve to accomplish at least one thing every day that will take you closer to the realization of your goal.

When you make progress you feel good about yourself; when you feel good about yourself, you make more progress, thus perpetuating a cycle of success. By focusing on your successes you amplify your energy and are more likely to remain in a positive, goal-oriented state that is conducive to success.

Focus solely on the critical issue

Sometimes you will experience a kind of slump, where your efforts feel sluggish and your progress seems to halt. When this happens, you need to think less about your methods, and concentrate instead on your desired results and purpose. Refocusing on your ultimate goal can help to renew your strength of purpose and can often get you unstuck. It also helps to review your plan; you should always be working from a detailed plan that outlines all of the steps that will lead you to your goal. If you are stuck, review the step on which you are working. Perhaps it needs to be broken down into smaller, more achievable goals. Do only one part of a step, and then another part, until you can proceed to the next step.

High achievers have a specific way of dealing with the obstacles or difficulties that confront them. When faced with a challenge, they typically put aside all irrelevant tasks and concentrate solely on the *critical issue*. The critical issue is the one task or problem that, upon completion, provides them with results that are greater than any other activity. Not only does this get them past the obstacle, but it also renews their sense of accomplishment and lends greater strength for the next challenge.

Do not panic if you cannot identify exactly what your next step should be. Remember that movement in any direction is preferable to inertia. Focus on solutions, not on problems. Once in motion, the critical issue will be revealed to you, and you will know exactly what you need to do next.

I have always found, when I was worrying, that the best thing to do was put my mind upon something, work hard and forget what was troubling me.

—THOMAS EDISON

Much energy is wasted on shifting between decisions, never quite choosing which path to take. Trying to decide what to do or when to do it saps the energy necessary to perform the task at hand. You know what needs to be done. You know when it is the *right time* to do it. Save the energy that you would spend vacillating between choices, and focus it all in one direction. You already know where you want to go, who you want to become, what you want to have. And you know how to get there.

High achievers also know that it is important to focus on what you are trying to accomplish, rather than on what you are trying to avoid. In their book *Leaders*, authors Warren Bennis and Burt Nanus discuss a concept they call the *Wallenda factor*, based on the famous tightrope aerialist Karl

Wallenda. Wallenda fell 75 feet to his death in 1978 while trying to walk a high wire suspended between two buildings in downtown San Juan, Puerto Rico. According to his wife, for three months prior to his fateful walk, all Wallenda thought about was *not falling*, rather than walking the tightrope. Bennis and Nanus concluded that when Wallenda put all his efforts into not falling, rather than walking the tightrope, he was destined to fall. The authors define the Wallenda factor as "the capacity to embrace positive goals, to pour one's energies into the task, not into looking behind and dredging up excuses for past events."

If you find yourself consumed with thoughts of what *might happen* if you don't reach your goal, focus instead on the positive goal of persevering until you achieve success. Do not be so consumed with preventing failure that you stumble right into it. Keep your mind focused on what will happen when you succeed, not on what will happen should you fail.

Staying focused on your goal will help you to persevere when adversity threatens to derail your progress. There is tremendous power in a focused mind, one that maintains a steady gaze on its desired outcome. By holding a vision of the finished work continuously in your mind's eye, a strength of purpose is born, providing the direction and energy needed to take you the distance to your goal.

Apply the effort, the results will follow

Direct your attention only to those things over which you have complete control. There are very few things that are within our complete control, but those things—particularly our attitudes and our efforts—have a tremendous impact on our lives. All of our energy should be directed toward our efforts, since we have complete control over how much effort we expend in the pursuit of our goal. If we apply the effort, the results will follow. It will always be tempting to work on peripheral tasks as they appear, but it is important to concentrate your efforts only toward the completion of the task at hand. Work on one task at a time, for as long as you can, then move on to the next.

Again and again, we will be tempted to stray from our course. The key to concentration is to maintain a *trifocal vision*. According to Dr. Roberto Assagioli, in *The Act of Will*, trifocal vision is the "...perception and retention in mind of the distant goal and purpose; the survey of the intermediate stages which extend from the point of departure to the arrival; and the awareness of the next step to be taken." Concentrate your focus on what to do next, review your direction, and rehearse in your mind the successful outcome. This will strengthen your resolve when faced with any obstacle.

> *That which we persist in doing becomes easier—not that the nature of the task has changed, but our ability to do has increased.*
> — EMERSON

When pursuing a challenging goal, high achievers focus their efforts in the direction required to obtain their goal until they have made all possible progress. They think of nothing else until they succeed in the one step that will allow them to proceed to the next, and so on. While it is important to remember the goal toward which you are working, too much preoccupation with the outcome can limit your ability to concentrate on the task at hand. Tension is created, inhibitions stifle creativity, and finally, anxiety takes over. Thinking about anything beyond the task at hand robs your current activity of its genius.

In his book, *Unlimit Your Life*, James Fadiman discusses the importance of concentrating on the task at hand: "It was said of Brother Lawrence, author of the medieval classic *The Practice of the Presence of God*, that although he never hurried and never worked quickly, he did twice as much work as any one else because *he always did exactly what needed to be done*. It is both a gift and a skill." You will conserve both time and energy by cultivating this ability.

Decide each day what is the most significant task that will lead to your goal, and put all of your resources into the accomplishment of this task. By making this a habit, it will quickly create a tremendous difference in your output. Don't worry too much about the finality of your decisions; there are very few decisions that are irrevocable. If you find yourself off course, simply refocus your attention back to your destination, put forth some effort, and you will turn yourself back in the right direction.

By staying focused on the work that faces you, obstacles are less likely to appear. Difficulties tend to arise when we are at rest—they seem to rush in to fill the void of our inactivity. When obstacles do appear, keep them in their proper perspective. You know where you are going, and how to get there, and you know exactly how to proceed. When you are focused, you overcome your problems as if they hardly exist. The ideal environment is one where you are spending most of your time and energy on the activities needed to achieve your goals, and much less time on problems that arise.

PUTTING LEVERAGE TO WORK IN YOUR LIFE

Success is achieved by the slow, incremental adding on of one day's labor to another's.

—GREGG LEVOY

Success is the accumulation of efforts

L everage, the practice of applying the sum of our progress toward the daily tasks at hand, has been called the secret weapon of the wealthy. Most people who have built their wealth will tell you that as they became richer, they were able to use their amassed wealth to gain further influence and opportunity, which in turn earned them more money. When used as a tool to reach your goals, leverage can enhance any program or plan. If you can learn to use leverage to your advantage, you will have learned the key to achieving optimum results. Leverage is an integral component of practically every significant accomplishment.

Leverage is created through the accumulation of small, single actions, repeated daily, whose benefits accrue over time, bringing positive results and a higher tolerance for adversity. Every milestone that you meet, every obstacle that you overcome on the path to your goal, leaves you with the strength and wisdom that you can draw on later. Operating from a position of strength brings with it the capacity to tolerate times of doubt, fear, and opposition.

Developing leverage requires you to focus less on your defeats and failures, and concentrate instead on parlaying the success you already have achieved into further success. The practice of leverage trusts that if you put in the effort to build on the things you are capable of doing well, the results will follow.

We often think of leverage as only a financial tool. It is much more than that. Leverage is a way of looking at the world and how we can make an impact on our lives through the development of our potential.

The Japanese have a principle called *Kaizen*, which is their equivalent of leverage. Simply put, *Kaizen* is the idea of gradual, simple improvements which, when added together over time, yield incredible results. The goal is to make daily improvement and progress, and to allow these results to compound themselves until we have achieved our ideal success.

> *I know of no more encouraging fact than the unquestionable ability of man to elevate his life by conscious endeavor.*
> — THOREAU

With *Kaizen*, the objective is to improve incrementally, to make steady progress, to not allow a single day to pass without having some kind of improvement take place. This may seem foreign to many of us who are accustomed to trying for the big breakthrough, the home run. By integrating *Kaizen* into our lives we stop trying to achieve success overnight and instead start on a gradual application of improvement in the quality of our lives.

Leverage maximizes your results

Even while pushing hard early in the pursuit of your goal, results tend to be small. As experience and practice accumulate, you will find that your results begin to skyrocket exponentially. You are working no harder, but the results are much greater. When you are able to apply the same effort, but find that your results are increasing, and your power and effectiveness are improving, then you are benefiting from leverage. It is developed over time with consistent effort and practice, and to use it effectively you must exercise it on a daily basis.

Ask yourself what action you could be taking on a regular basis that would contribute the most toward your goal. There will always be at least one thing you do well that will give you immediate benefits. Find that one thing and begin to build on it.

Your progress will be in direct proportion to your efforts, and the amount of effort that you exert is entirely up to you. Concentrating in one area in which you are competent can, over time, produce improvements beyond anything you can probably imagine. The key is to focus on one thing at a time. If we spread ourselves out working on a number of different projects and tasks simultaneously, we disperse our attention and lose the ability to leverage our efforts.

Applying the principles of leverage toward your goals will, over time, maximize your results and help you to reach your goals in the shortest time possible. Without leverage, you can only do the work of one person. With leverage, you can perform the work of many.

WORKING THROUGH THE FATIGUE BARRIER

Look well into yourself; there is a source of strength which will always spring up if you will always look there.

—MARCUS AURELIUS

Learn your limits, then surpass them

All of us have a fatigue barrier that, when reached, halts our activity. Is this the time to take a break? How much further could we go if we would only work through our fatigue? Probably a lot further, much further than we think. Most of us know little about our own physical and mental limits. We allow past experience to dictate when we should stop, reaching a point of fatigue that we recognize and then quitting. Some types of work do require a fresh mind or body, but most tasks will not suffer from an exerted effort applied while working through your fatigue. If we rested every time we became tired, we would accomplish very little.

Psychologist and philosopher William James made this point about fatigue: "If an unusual necessity forces us onward, a surprising thing occurs. The fatigue gets worse up to a certain point, when, gradually or suddenly, it passes away and we are fresher than before!" This he attributes to having tapped a new level of energy. James felt that there may be "layer after layer of this experience, a third and fourth *wind*." We have found "...amounts of ease and power that we never dreamed ourselves to own, sources of strength habitually not taxed, because habitually we never punch through the obstruction of fatigue."

As long as you are making progress, you are succeeding. If today you cannot achieve one hundred percent of the results you were working toward, that's okay. Even as you are winding down your day's activities, always try to push just a bit more, reach out a little farther. Try to improve today's results by another percentage point, perhaps two or three. Sometimes you'll find that when you thought you were at a stopping point, you break through the fatigue barrier and find the energy to continue.

It is said that Albert Schweitzer used to plunge his feet into cold water to keep himself awake and alert during the night while studying for medical school. All high achievers can and do work through fatigue, no matter what it takes. They get tired and keep going. It's okay to take a break, to rest. But then get back to it. Know that the energy you need will present itself when you need it most. If you keep working, you will find a way to finish. Many highly successful people have claimed that they tend to finish stronger than they began, echoing William James' comments.

Fatigue makes cowards of us all.

—VINCE LOMBARDI

Anyone can overcome fatigue

Endurance athletes have come to know that the human mind and body are capable of rather extraordinary feats. Contrary to what most of us think, our mental resolve tends to fail us long before our body gives up. We may feel some physical discomfort, but it usually passes if we can muster up the mental strength to weather the storm.

Long distance runners talk of experiencing a *high* after

prolonged periods of running. The latest scientific evidence suggests the presence of natural hormones, called beta endorphins, that are secreted into the body to counter pain. These hormones are capable of producing a very real feeling of euphoria that can facilitate the creative process. Anyone—not just an athlete—is capable of achieving this sensation. By continuing your work beyond the initial stages of fatigue, your body will make the adjustments necessary to get you through to the end.

Stopping at the first signs of fatigue can quickly develop into an unwanted habit. There is a natural tendency to stop and rest at the initial onset of weariness. To combat this habit, try the following:

- Make a conscious effort to keep going. Learn what true fatigue feels like by staying with your task.

- Take note of any new sensations and how your body compensates. Use this awareness to keep yourself from dwelling on the discomfort you feel.

- When you feel like quitting, reverse the thought process by replacing your *quitter* thoughts with images of your goal.

- Relax and breathe deeply. Consider this a time-out.

With practice, you will create a pattern that can be repeated the next time you reach your fatigue barrier, and each time, it will become easier to continue.

Noted mountain climber, author, and motivational speaker John R. Noe believes that it is "…a common misconception that hard work is the most exhausting human activity. Actually, the greatest energy-sapper most of us ever face is emotional fatigue." We often become worn out *before* beginning many tasks because we needlessly allow anxiety take its toll.

If most fatigue is a creation of the mind, then the mind can also defeat it. This does not mean that the banishment of mental fatigue is easy, but rather that it is possible if you recognize it and make the effort to continue. Fatigue is simply an obstacle that is overcome with determination and perseverance. When you have learned to work through your fatigue barrier, you will become infinitely more productive and your progress will flourish.

REST OFTEN, QUIT NEVER

*It is one of the illusions that the present hour
is not the critical decisive hour.*

—Thomas Carlyle

Rest long enough to regroup

While it is often necessary to take a break from the hard work put forth in pursuit of your goals, rest only long enough to regroup and refocus your energy. Resting for too long can lessen the gains you have made, as well as hamper your future ability to make gains. If you spend too much time away from the pursuit of your goals you risk the loss of the leverage you have created.

The frequency and duration of rest periods will fluctuate with each of us. Decide what schedule works best for you. If long and infrequent breaks seem to be the most effective for you, then allow yourself these. If you prefer shorter, more frequent breaks, then follow this schedule instead.

A common technique employed by peak performers is the practice of *little and often*; making steady progress while taking frequent breaks to conserve energy. By taking small, easy steps you can maintain a feeling of confidence and a sense of control that are vital for the long term. Whatever the pace you choose to set, try and perform as well as you can, for as long as you can. Rest when you need to, and then get back to it. Do not be afraid of hard work; no one has ever drowned in sweat from working too hard, and it's not likely that you will be the first.

How long or hard you work at something is up to you. It is not always necessary to apply the maximum effort; some prefer to work at a more leisurely pace toward their goals, depending on the timeline they have set for themselves. What's important is to do what works best for you. Try different methods until you find the environment that is most conducive to your personal achievement.

Never quit in your pursuit. Never give up the chase. By remaining active—notwithstanding periods of rest—you will make gains, develop leverage, and make larger gains. Temporary setbacks will interrupt your progress, but with a commitment towards a significant goal, you can and will prevail.

Laziness is nothing more than the habit of resting before you get tired.
—JULES RENARD

When adversity strikes, a break is sometimes in order. Taking a break from your work can offer a new perspective that allows you to overcome the obstacles that block your path. Writer Gregg Levoy says that "...one of the tasks of perseverance is knowing when to stop persevering, to simply drop everything and take a break. It is a discipline all its own."

Do not sacrifice necessary periods of rest, thinking you will reach your goal sooner. Often when we are unable to obtain our goal in a short period of time, we become frustrated and quit. Successful goal achievers understand that it is preferable and sometimes necessary to take an extended break from their work in order to avoid feelings of frustration that might lead them to quit altogether.

Your rest should be free from stress

We all need vacations, both for their rejuvenating powers and to give us something to look forward to. The ideal situation is to love what you do so much that it feels as though you are always on vacation. Sometimes we will take a vacation involving travel and being away from our home and work for extended periods. Other times we will just take brief vacations at home, putting aside our work until we are reenergized. Often we simply take a time out during the day when things just don't feel right for us. These breaks are a necessary part of goal attainment. The important thing to remember is not to rest too long or too often. Momentum gained can be lost when efforts to maintain it are not made.

> *The way to greatness is the path of self-reliance, independence and steadfastness in time of trial and stress.*
>
> —HERBERT HOOVER

Your rest should be free from stress, or it isn't rest at all. A good rule to follow is to work when you work, and rest when you rest. By mixing the two, the results of both will suffer. Despite missing time from work, upon your return, you will be energized and capable of producing at an even greater pace. The well-disciplined person knows when a break is in order and then takes it. Learn how to pace yourself for maximum results; this is one of the keys to perseverance.

Setbacks will test your resolve

You will always find a way to get what you want as long as you never give up. Setbacks will challenge your commitment. You will discover just how important your goals are when you begin to face the inevitable adversity. There will be bouts of strife that will test your resolve in ways previously unimagined. But it is not necessary to suffer from these periods of adversity; rather, each hurdle that you over-come will strengthen your will to succeed.

Focus on your strengths, rather than your weaknesses. Look for ways to make things happen, not for reasons why they won't work. Search for opportunities, not excuses; don't quit at the first sign of difficulty and then blame your fail-ure on external factors. Look within for the strength needed to get you through the tough times.

We all possess a tremendous potential to pursue our goals; we are all equally capable of focusing on a goal and apply-ing the effort necessary to get there. Where we differ is in the amount of desire we possess to begin and to continue the pursuit. You must dig deep within your potential, to draw out the power of your resolve. This power will keep you so busy working toward your goals that you will hardly have time to become sidetracked by problems and obstacles. Peak performers develop the personal power needed to obtain their goals and they focus exclusively on the tasks that lead to those goals.

CHAPTER 6

Operating In A *Tastes Good* Environment

PERSEVERANCE OCCURS NATURALLY IN THE CORRECT ENVIRONMENT

*To succeed...we must create circumstances
which maximize our opportunities to
achieve, excel, and get ahead...*

—DON BEVERIDGE

The steps to your goal must excite you

The success of any significant goal hinges on your ability to create an environment that maximizes your effectiveness. The tasks leading to your goal must *taste good.* That is, we must pursue goals that are made up of steps that interest and excite us. We can only persevere when striving for results that transcend our current station, and we will only be motivated to struggle when the work is challenging and stimulating.

The high level of energy that it takes to achieve our goals demands that we be interested in the pursuit. While some measure of the work may be tedious and uninteresting, it's imperative that our goals are made up of steps that will inspire us and create the drive and desire necessary to bring about success.

This is not as difficult as it may sound, even for people who think that any kind of hard work is distasteful. If your goal is important to you, and if the desire to reach it is intense enough, then most of the steps that lead to its attainment will *taste good* to you.

Confront the difficult while it is still easy; accomplish the great by a series of small acts.
—Tao Te Ching

Develop your inner resolve

Creating a *tastes good* environment requires that you develop the inner resolve that is essential for change. One of the first steps you take should be to eliminate activities in your life that are not in some way helping you to achieve your goals. This does not mean giving up the things that are necessary to your health and general welfare, including some leisure and social time. But in order to pursue your goals with the effort and energy that is necessary, you may have to sacrifice some time that is normally spent doing other things. Learn how to control and manipulate your environment so that you make the greatest use of the time that you have every day.

If a task is distasteful to you, you will not give it the attention it needs to be completed. Seek an alternate task that will deliver the same results. A common suggestion offered by weight training instructors is to eliminate all exercises that you don't enjoy, and replace them with ones that still work the same muscle group. If you are working muscles with lifts that you don't like or are bored with, you will find excuses to not do the lift and the muscle group gets neglected. In this case, you should find another more engaging way to work the same muscle group. It is possible to create a set of tasks that are wholly enjoyable to us, and still produce the results we need.

What makes an environment conducive to goal-related activities? A healthy environment for generating success is one that creates and maximizes the circumstances that will allow you to persevere through adversity. You must have a healthy physical and emotional environment for success. Look within yourself, contemplate your environment, and learn how to dominate it, for anyone who does not control their environment will never be successful.

To develop and maintain an environment that is conducive to the facilitation of your goals, you must learn:

- That there is always enough time to do what's important.

- How to work in the midst of the big fear—the fear of failure.

- When you have committed a false start—know when it's time to quit.

- How to create and maintain a *tastes good* environment.

When our goals reflect what it is we truly desire, there should be no conflict between what we want to do and what we need to do. This then is the essence of a *tastes good* environment; our goals mirror our desires and our actions lead to our goals. It's like being on a diet that consists only of foods that we enjoy. There is little need for self-discipline since the things we *want* to be doing are the things we *should* be doing. Perseverance will come naturally in such an environment.

We should always be in pursuit of the set of circumstances that we can control and dominate. Some ventures we simply survive; in other areas we thrive. Always look to drop out of projects that inhibit or otherwise break your spirit. Look instead for arenas that will bring out your best. Create those opportunities that you need to build a successful life. Success means getting what you want out of life by creating an environment that allows you to do those things you want to do, when you want to do them.

THERE IS ALWAYS TIME TO DO WHAT'S IMPORTANT

*No road is too long for the man who advances
deliberately and without undue haste; and no
honors are too distant for the man who prepares
himself for them with patience.*

—BRUYERE

Winners understand that success takes time

One of the primary differences between winners and losers is that winners understand that success takes time. They know that they may have to start at the entry level and spend perhaps years moving up to where they aspire to be. Most people, however, want fast returns relative to the amount of effort and time they put in. Without an understanding of how much time it will take to complete your project, you may become easily frustrated and give up on your goal when it seems to be taking too long to accomplish.

Your greatest efforts will rarely bring immediate results. An acute awareness of the time it will take to reach your goal can strengthen your resolve to never quit. Armed with the knowledge that all significant achievements take time, you will be more likely to sustain your efforts over a longer period of time. Common sense tells us that the more time we invest in our goal, the greater the results will be.

The realization of any major goal will require a significant investment of time. Do not become disillusioned when you don't succeed on the very first try. We often are frustrated by sloppy or slow beginnings because our impatient egos tell us that we should be able to master a skill with little or no practice. When our initial attempts to succeed at a task are thwarted by misjudgments or mistakes, we stop trying, so as not to embarrass ourselves. This is a trait that is solely unique to adults—children rarely display this type of inhibition. Rather, a child, though equally prone to mistakes and frustration, will work seemingly endlessly until they master climbing a set of stairs, riding a bicycle, or whatever new skill they have set their sights on. As adults, we can learn a lot from the persistence displayed by a child who is focused on succeeding.

The method of the enterprising is to plan with audacity, and execute with vigor; to sketch out a map of possibilities; and then to treat them as probabilities.
—CHRISTIAN BOVEE

Patience is persistence in action

Patience is nothing more than persistence in action, and is a required tool for any high achiever. Exercising patience in the pursuit of a goal requires wisdom, maturity, and integrity. When you are patient, you are secure in the knowledge that success takes time, and that you will succeed if only you take the time that is required.

Most of the results we achieve in any endeavor occur only after repeated efforts over an extended period of time. You may be tempted to give up much too soon, before your efforts have had time to bring you measurable results. The only way to counter this is to have a steadfast confidence in your goal and in your ability to reach your goal—you must have an unrelenting belief that with time, effort, and perseverance, you will eventually reach your goal.

Do the hard work first

The initial progress that we gain from our efforts is very satisfying. After that our progress levels off naturally. It's at this point that we tend to look for the big gains, and when we fail to see them, we become discouraged, which can curtail our efforts and further delay results. At these times we must recognize that the rewards of our efforts are sometimes intangible, but each day that we work toward our goal, we are gaining the strength and confidence we will need to overcome adversity. It can take a long time to reach the level where your efforts produce discernible results every day.

Patience isn't a virtue when it comes to getting results; it's a necessity.
—ROBERT RINGER

Seeking and expecting immediate results creates excessive anxiety and inhibits your creative energy. The search for immediate gratification can kill your dream. Dr. M. Scott Peck, in *The Road Less Traveled*, believes delaying gratification "…is a process of scheduling the pain and pleasure of life in such a way as to enhance the pleasure by meeting and experiencing the pain first and getting it over with. It is the only decent way to live."

By doing the hard work first, you put yourself in a position to better enjoy the benefits from your efforts. What's more common is to put off the most difficult work until last. But the more we avoid them, the more difficult the tasks looming before us seem to become. Soon the pursuit of our goal is blocked by obstacles that appear insurmountable, and we quit.

If you are not getting the results you want in the time you have allowed, do not become discouraged. Instead, reevaluate your timetable and make adjustments, allowing as long as you need for the completion of each task. Keep moving forward. Unless you must meet certain immovable deadlines, you can stay with a project as long as you like, for as long as it takes. Don't let a preconceived notion of how long it *should* take cause you to give up too soon. Get in the practice of periodically reevaluating the time and resources it will take you to reach your goal, and change your deadlines accordingly. This keeps you from constantly feeling that you are behind schedule, which can lead to a pessimistic attitude.

You will never find the time to do everything that you want to do, but there will always be enough time to do what's important. Failing to accurately assess how much time is needed to reach your goal often results in trying to accomplish more work in a particular period of time than your skill level will allow. This leads to sloppy, unfinished work, frustration, and failure to meet preestablished deadlines. Not meeting a deadline can cause you to give up entirely on your goal. It is essential that your plan contain an accurate and fair assessment of the time needed to complete each step.

Rarely is any major project finished in the time initially scheduled. You will not be the first person to miss a deadline. The key to success does not mean you have to meet all prearranged deadlines, but rather to stay with your goal, no matter how long it takes. If your goal is worthy and realistic, there is no reason why you should quit. Plans and timetables are easily corrected, and as you gain experience you will become more accurate in estimating the amount of time a particular task will take.

Another hazard that halts progress is the belief that every problem must be solved immediately when it arises. Often a problem comes up that has no obvious or immediate solution. When this happens, learn as much as you can about your problem and then put it aside. Some problems must lie unresolved for a while until your subconscious has had some time to work on the solution. High achievers all seem to possess a strong tolerance for ambiguity. They are able to make a non-decision; that is, when they cannot decide exactly what to do, they resolve not to decide, at least not right away. You must be able to put aside some problems and focus on other tasks, confident in the knowledge that the solution will eventually present itself to you.

The secret of success is constancy of purpose.
—Benjamin Disraeli

Effective time management is a key ingredient to success. We all possess the same 24 hours in a day, the same 7 days in a week, the same 52 weeks in a year—but some of us manage to accomplish great amounts of work with our time, while others do very little. If you use your time wisely, it can become your ally. With a concerted effort and an unwavering focus, time will bring you the progress and results that will eventually lead to the realization of your greatest goals.

SURVIVING IN THE LAP OF FEAR

For as children tremble and fear everything in the blind darkness, so we in the light sometimes fear what is no more to be feared than the things children in the dark hold in terror and imagine will come true.

—LUCRETIUS

Beware of the fear of failure

Pursuing our goals is terrifying. Anytime we venture into the unknown it becomes easy to talk ourselves into a state of paralyzing inaction. All big dreams and great accomplishments have fears attached to them. Fear is the greatest obstacle that you will encounter en route to your success. But if your desire to succeed is strong enough, your fears will never be greater than your commitment to your goals.

One of the most paralyzing fears that you will encounter is the fear of failure. Fear is a physiological reaction to a psychological interpretation of an event or situation. It's important to understand your fears, because how you view an event or situation is how you will react to it. If you are afraid of failure, you will tend to avoid situations where there exists a possibility of failure. But where you find the greatest risk of failure will also contain the greatest opportunities to succeed.

According to freelance writer Gregg Levoy, "... we have become conditioned to avoiding what is fearful." At an emotional level, the logic is impeccable, because if "...we don't try, then we don't have to be afraid, and we can console ourselves that even if none of our dreams come true, then at least neither will our nightmares...avoidance becomes its own reward." If we give it our best, and come up short, what does that say about us? Most of us would rather not find out.

Are you afraid to try because you have risked and lost in the past? Are you convinced that you cannot succeed now, because of previous mistakes? *At any time in your life* you can resolve to unlearn the lessons of your past and reenter the arena, armed with a renewed confidence in your abilities and a strong desire to persevere. Achieving worthwhile goals requires an effort that can only come from a fully committed application.

Drs. Robert Kriegel and Marilyn Harris Kriegel have written extensively on peak performance. In their book, *The C Zone*, they explain what happens when you become fearful: "...your mind plays tricks on you when you are afraid. Remote improbabilities appear as realistic possibilities. Fear distorts your perception, making situations look more dangerous and difficult than they really are, while your ability to handle them appears diminished." Fear has the power to turn your environment hostile while simultaneously rendering you powerless. This combination can stifle even the most resourceful people.

> *While one person hesitates because he feels inferior, the other is busy making mistakes and becoming superior.*
> —HENRY C. LINK

Fearing failure, we delay beginning. In this state, you are less likely to take action. While action is the only cure, it is also what you are fear the most. A state of inaction eventually causes us to stop thinking about what *could* be and start accepting things the way they *are*, no matter how dissatisfied we are with the present situation.

One of the most common and useless fears is the fear of looking bad in front of others. Fear of *losing face* keeps even the most motivated people from trying new things. All highly successful people know that the road to achievement is littered with their mistakes. People who set only safe, easy goals because they are afraid of looking bad will always come up short in the end, having removed any chance for success.

> *The way of a superior man is threefold: virtuous, he is free from anxieties; wise, he is free from perplexities; bold, he is free from fear.*
>
> —CONFUCIUS

Self-awareness is the tool that identifies when we are focusing on our fears. The fear of failure works at a level of our subconscious, and we respond to this fear by sabotaging our efforts. The fear of failure is so prevalent that it can prevent you from moving forward, yet so subtle you never even know you are being influenced by it. Some of your fears are based on actual memories of your past failures. Other fears are imaginary, projections of future events that will probably never occur. Instead of projecting your fear into the future, try imagining a more positive outcome, one in which your goals are readily achieved. We must refrain from acting on our fears if we are to put forth our best efforts toward achieving our goals.

Counter your fears with courage

If we can learn to manage our fears, we can set our goals high—and reach them. We will never eliminate fear. It is as instinctive to us as is hunger. But just as we can abate our hunger by eating, we can counter our fears with confident actions and perseverance. The price of success always involves facing significant fears, and working through them.

Courage can be defined as strength of character, as the power to do the right thing rather than the instinctive thing. Anyone can be courageous, anytime they desire, as often as they like. And just as endurance is developed, so is courage; each time you exercise it, you reinforce your confidence and make it more likely that you will face your fears the next time you are confronted by them. If repeated enough, acting with courage becomes a successful habit, just as backing down when you are afraid often becomes a conditioned response.

Confidence is the big secret of success...the mind, not the body, is the limit.

—ARNOLD SCHWARZENEGGER

You can only learn this response by practicing it. Again and again you must choose to be bold and do what it is that you fear. At first you will have to force yourself to act with courage. Do it anyway— it will always be worth the effort. Remember, where there is fear, there is also power to face and overcome the fear.

Consider what you fear the most. Is it public speaking? What about crowds? Some people are terrified of talking to people they don't know, yet others make a living calling strangers every day. Many of us are afraid of heights, yet others spend much of their lives climbing mountains. Whatever you fear, there is always someone who is doing that very thing right now, in spite of any fear. How can we take this knowledge and turn it into an advantage for us? First, accept that if some activity you fear is being accomplished by someone else, then you can do it as well. Second, remember that courage is the conquest of fear, so there can be no courage if you are not first afraid.

Cultivate your courage, and learn to rely on it when you are most afraid; it is a powerful ally. Progress involves discovering the courage within, stepping out into the light and staying there. Accept that things will go wrong. Accept that there will be setbacks and that you will experience fear—real fear—every day. You must be willing to stake everything on your abilities.

> *Live daringly, boldly, fearlessly. Taste the relish to be found in competition—in having to put forth the best within you.*
>
> —HENRY KAISER

Feelings of fear can, in some instances, be an asset. You can use the adrenaline that fear produces to your advantage by directing it toward the attainment of your goal. Facing fear creates an opportunity to grow and renew your strength; strive to learn from it. Look for opportunities to be brave. Seek to be courageous. Search out situations that require you to put forth your stronger self. Only in times of adversity will you learn how powerful you really are.

High achievers succeed not because they are fearless, but because they face their fears and move forward. Trying to evade your fears instead of facing them produces problems that weaken your resolve and create self-doubt. Considerable energy is expended on avoidance, leaving little for the work that is necessary to achieve your goal. Anytime you leave your fears unresolved, they continue to plague you and can spoil any other activities in which you are engaged.

Where do we gather the necessary strength to move through

our fears and maintain action toward our goals? Our strength comes from courage that is born of a strong commitment to a worthy goal. Without an unbending commitment, it is doubtful that we will be able to overcome our fears and persevere to the attainment of our goals.

Courage is taking action in spite your fears. Courage gives you strength of character, a high tolerance to ambiguity, and the capacity to withstand extreme difficulties. Once you discover the power of your courage, you can always draw on it. If you are determined to reach your goals no matter what, you will find the strength and the courage to get there.

Action ignites the power that resides in us all

Our memories contain the best, and worst, of our achievements. From our memories we can draw on our courageous acts to boost our confidence; reliving past victories can give us a strength and confidence that is immeasurable. At the same time, the past can fill us with memories of loss and failure. We all have memories of fears, both real and imagined, that can influence our actions without our conscious awareness. The fear of repeating past mistakes often keeps us from acting in the present. We need to counter these fears with thoughts of success and feelings of confidence.

One way to ease into your fears is to arrange your tasks in such a way as to create a steady accumulation of achievements, so that you always have a successful effort behind you. Spend your time and energy focusing on your existing success instead of on your failures and losses. Each new success adds to your previous successes. This in turn will build your confidence and instill you with courage.

Try starting small, by putting yourself in only moderately fearful situations. As you develop some confidence, move on to more difficult tasks. By approaching your fears slowly and deliberately, you avoid becoming paralyzed by the sum of all your fears, which can be overwhelming. Resolve to conquer your fears one fear at a time. You will gradually develop a tolerance to operating in the presence of fear.

...act with confidence beyond the range of familiar beacons.

—JOSEPH SCHUMPETER

The secret to overcoming fear is to focus on what you want, rather than on what you fear. Fear begets fear, and if you focus on it, it will defeat you, because your motive will be only to escape your fear. Look instead to what you want, concentrate on your goal, and let your desire for success drive you. Trust yourself, move forward in spite of your fear, with the faith that you will succeed if only you work at it long enough.

Confidence is an important trait to nurture; if we *expect* to win, we will win more often than if we expect to lose. After a setback, it is essential that you regain your confidence. Make a list—mental or written—of what you learned, and decide what you will do differently next time. Reward yourself for not giving up, and immediately begin working toward the next challenge. Dwelling on the errors you made will only reinforce them. By learning your lessons and applying them to future efforts, you create a win/win exchange where even defeat offers invaluable rewards.

Failure is caused by actions we do not take—not by the actions we do take. We fail when we don't act, when we allow our fears to force us to quit, or worse, to never begin.

Approach all of your goal activities with the attitude that it's better to lose while trying than to lose by default. Take care of what is in front of you regardless of your fears. Be more afraid of never getting a chance to chase your goals than at failing in the attempt to reach them.

When you interpret your results negatively, and allow defeat to suggest that you are a loser, then you will often act like a loser. Losers never expect to win, and are seldom disappointed. Winners, on the other hand, know that defeat is only part of the process; they know that if they persevere and keep fighting, they will eventually win. They know they may lose often before they win, and they view losses as the stepping stones that will lead them closer to their eventual success.

Everyone has talent. What is rare is the courage to follow the talent to the dark place where it leads.

—ERICA JONG

If you can counter your fears with courageous action, then nothing will be beyond your reach. High achievers face the same obstacles that you do, but they have the confidence to act in the face of those obstacles, whatever they may be. They know fear is simply another barrier to be overcome, and that no fear is great enough to stop someone who has at their defense the desire, courage, and perseverance to work on until they have attained their goals.

FALSE START...OR TIME TO QUIT?

Failure exists only in the grave. Man, being alive, hath not yet failed; always he may turn about and ascend by the same path he descended by...

—Frederick Van Rensselaer Day

Move on when necessary

Is it ever okay to quit, to give up on your goal? Does quitting always mean you have failed? While it's important to know when to stop, to recognize when enough is enough, we have a responsibility to ourselves to be sure we have done all we are capable of. We need to recognize when the effort or resources we are expending are no longer worthy of the results we are receiving. If we have chosen a goal that we are just not going to reach, the sooner we recognize and accept this fact, the sooner we can start pursing a new goal. The decision to stop working toward your goal should always be a personal one, and should always be made on the basis of the facts and figures, not on emotion alone.

There is a common expression in the business world: *stop throwing good money after bad.* When a venture is heading nowhere, it might become necessary to prevent further losses and get out before it gets any worse. Apply the same principle to your own goals. Although you may have invested a considerable amount of time, money, and effort, if it seems there is no longer any hope left, you should stop wasting further resources, learn what you can, and move on. Regard these *failures* for what they are, goals that didn't work out—but never allow them to discourage you from setting and pursuing new goals.

We must maintain the flexibility to alter our goals—or at least our plans—if we determine that the results we are seeking are no longer attainable. We should not be so inflexible that we allow our goals to imprison us in activities or behaviors that are detrimental to ourselves or others. Goal attainment requires a clarity of mind and purpose that allows us to distinguish between achievable goals and futile efforts. Successful people spend considerable time making ing sure the goals they choose are sound and worthy; when the path becomes difficult, they may change their approach as *Men are made strong not* needed, but rarely quit in its pursuit. *by winning easy battles,*

There will be a number of forks on the *but by losing hard-fought* path to your goal where you will have the choice to either quit or you find the *ones.* strength to carry on. If you decide to quit, —DICK BASS then only you can determine if you have failed or not. If you are able to salvage some significant lessons from your projects, and apply these lessons to future endeavors, then you haven't failed. If you come out of it with nothing more save the strengthening of your resolve, then you *definitely* haven't failed. But only you can decide, and you will know if your decision to quit was based on wisdom and facts, or if you were simply unable or unwilling to persevere.

The realization of a significant goal always involves overcoming some adversity. Never make the decision to quit during desperate times; problems typically appear worse than they really are. Sometimes, though, repeated obstacles and setbacks might indicate that you are in pursuit of something that is simply not possible for you to have, or that your plan is faulty. Draw on your wisdom to determine what your next step should be.

Be certain of the virtue of your goal; it is counterproductive and time consuming to work long and hard in the wrong direction. Do not give up on a worthy goal because your plan is faulty; if you stick with your goal long enough to try another approach, you will succeed. Ask the following questions, and make adjustments as needed:

- Are you working hard enough?
- Are you working too hard?
- Can you still visualize the attainment of your goal?
- Have you gotten any closer to your goal since you started?

Know when to change direction

It is important to have the presence of mind to recognize a false start for what it is. Rather than signaling the futility of our goal, a false start may simply indicate that you need to continue in a new direction toward the same goal. By carefully monitoring our progress and referring to our plan, we can tell when we have made such a false start, and the sooner we discover this, the sooner we can get back on track. One sign that you are on the wrong path is when you are not able to muster any enthusiasm for the tasks in front of you. Another sign is when you find yourself working unendingly on the same task, with little or no results. At these times, it is helpful to review your plan and adjust your course as necessary.

Be realistic in the assessment of your progress. Honestly examine what is going wrong and make sure you address every issue. Do not give up on your goal simply because you have not yet found the means to get there. If you possess the desire to reach your goal, and if your goal is worthy, you also possess the ability to get there. Be prepared to modify, replace, or otherwise alter your original plan. Even the most successful people will tell you that they had numerous false starts before they found the correct combination of methods that worked just right for them.

MAINTAINING A TASTES GOOD ENVIRONMENT

Keep expectations alive. Keep nourishing them...
The trick is to moderate your strength and knowledge
and advance little by little toward success.

—BALTASAR GRACIAN

Dealing with partial goal attainment

Your dreams should be as grand and as bold as you can imagine them; setting and pursuing significant goals allows you to obtain greater results than ever. Achieving only part of our dream is much more satisfying than succeeding at a more modest goal that we cared little about, and it is always preferable to never setting any goals at all. Ask any person who has had an exercise or weight loss program if they achieved all they had hoped for. They may or may not be achieving all of the fitness goals they initially set, but the physical and mental benefits of their progress are better than if they remained in a sedentary lifestyle.

How do we deal with partial attainment of our goals? Should we feel bad because we failed to hit the mark? It's important to remember that our goals and aspirations are fluid, not static. The outcomes we choose for ourselves will change as we pursue them. Reaching only part of our goal is okay, as long as we believe it is.

Suppose you are a runner, and you decide that you want to enter a 10k race. Your goal is to finish your race in 50 minutes or less. You develop and follow a training program. Now you are training with a purpose, a goal. Your progress is tracked and examined. The race is marked on your calendar and your training schedule is tailored to have you in the best possible condition on race day. You have a plan and you follow it faithfully. Everything goes smoothly.

Race day arrives and you run a good race. Your time, however, is 51 minutes, one minute slower than your goal. Should you consider this a failure? Should you berate yourself for not training more vigorously, or for not pushing harder during the race? Peak performers would recognize a time of 51 minutes as a success. They would consider missing a goal by only two percent as acceptable, probably as very good. They would feel positive about the progress made and would use their finishing time as a guide for setting their next goal. The most important thing that a peak performer would do at this point is to immediately set a new goal for the next race—a new race, a faster time, more progress. The original goal, to run a 10k race in 50 minutes or less, should not be abandoned; in fact, at 51 minutes, you are closer than ever to your goal.

When you are aspiring to the highest place, it is honorable to reach the second or even the third rank.

—Cicero

Remember that you should always be in pursuit of progress, not perfection. Make progress toward your dreams everyday. A little progress is always preferable to a lot of inaction.

Beware of the bad day

Making progress on our good days is easy. We wake up refreshed and seem to have all the answers. No adjustments are necessary on days like these. We feel full of energy and creativity. We make plans for the day, accomplish all or most of the tasks in front of us, and end the day with a feeling of contentment and control. If all of our days went like this we would achieve many more of the goals we set for ourselves.

The bad days, however, are entirely different. They start out badly and seem to get progressively worse. We lose our keys. We forget things. We're late to meetings. We're tired and unmotivated. We feel lucky if we get through the day at all.

> *The person who makes a success of living is the one who sees his goal steadily and aims for it unswervingly.*
> —CECIL B. DeMILLE

We all have bad days. What needs to change is how we respond to them. Instead of allowing a bad day to start a downward spiral that leads to more bad days, make your bad day just one in the midst of many, many good days. Do not allow yourself to feel bad any longer than necessary. When we feel bad, we see only obstacles, and when we see obstacles, we lose momentum. Loss of momentum creates more obstacles, and so on. The obstacles seem larger than life, looming ahead like an insurmountable barrier. There will be little if any progress made once this negative cycle has begun.

One bad day can cause us to give up our efforts entirely, if we allow it to turn into a series of bad days, which becomes a bad week, a bad month, and so forth. Anyone who has tried to maintain a healthy diet understands this. A bad day can cause you to go off your diet, *just for one day*, which can easily lead to another day off the diet, and another, until all of the progress that you made is lost. You can even end up worse off than you were before you started. This happens in all sorts of goal-achieving activities.

How can you prevent this from happening? First, approach each day as the most important day yet. Maintain a focus on the tasks facing you on that day only, without allowing yourself to become overwhelmed by the big *picture*. Second, accept the fact that sometimes you are just going to have to continue when you don't feel like it. The ability to make progress on days we don't feel *up to task* is what separates the average person from the high achiever. Finally, resolve that when you wake up feeling bad, you will do all you can to salvage the day. Work one more hour than you planned to. Do one more task than you want to. Make something of your day, every day.

Starting over again, daily

Many of us are in the habit of starting and stopping in the pursuit of our goals, over and over again. We try to accomplish something, make some progress, and then we quit. Sometimes we quit slowly, not even noticing it until we look up one day and realize that we haven't made any progress on our goals in a long time. Then we start again, perhaps months later, having to repeat the same work we did earlier. Little is accomplished by this method.

Unless we start doing things differently, we will continue to get the same mediocre results. We must start over on our goals every day, beginning fresh every morning, with a renewed commitment and focus. By reminding ourselves every day what our goal is and what must be done to get there, we can keep ourselves from drifting away from the work at hand. Look at each task before you as new, fresh, and full of excitement.

The beginning of your day is critical. How you begin your day can very well determine how you will conduct your life. Of course, if you fail to begin your day in a positive way, you can always turn it around at any point and become more positive and productive. Each and every moment brings with it the opportunity to start again fresh, unencumbered by the previous moment. Every moment is an opportunity for self-renewal.

It's no secret that the harder you work, the greater are your rewards. If you spend most of your time talking about your goals rather than working toward them, they will remain elusive. You must resolve to keep moving forward and to never give up, and you must make this resolution every day, without fail.

By making each day the most important day of your life, by doing all you possibly can toward the attainment of your goals, tomorrow will always take care of itself. Treat today as if you are being judged by today only. Start every day free of all past transgressions, carrying forward only successes and victories, as well as the lessons you have learned so far. Recommit to your goals every day, resolve to be productive and positive, and you will be rewarded with success.